Seeing Stars

Memoirs of a Freelance
Celebrity Articles Writer

Shirley Lee Ames

With Pictures by Ralph Merlino

Published in the USA by:
BearManor Media
P O Box 71426
Albany, Georgia 31708
www.bearmanormedia.com

ISBN 978-1-59393-628-0

Printed in the United States of America.

Book and cover design by Darlene Swanson of Van-garde Imagery, Inc.

Dedication

This book is dedicated to the memory of my very dear, talented and hard-working husband, Bob, and my loving parents, Nina and Gene. I also dedicate the book to my two sons, David and Jeffrey, my daughters-in-law, Marion and Cecilia, my grandsons, Garrett and Nicholas, and my cousin Jill.

With Special Thanks to Ralph, who shared many of these adventures and took the pictures, to my friend Barbara, who gave me advice and encouragement, and to all the Stars who allowed me to write about them.

Contents

Preface

I've never thought of myself as a "people person," but I guess, in some ways, I am.

I dislike parties of any kind and couldn't bring myself to schmooze if my life depended on it.

On the other hand, I've had a 40-plus-years professional writing career dealing with a wide range of topics that include travel, business, collectibles, horses and other animals, general information, children's and young people's self-help articles and fiction stories, and even, more recently, the military.

But the larger share of my published articles have dealt with profiles and at-homes about well known actors and actresses of motion pictures and television. This book tells of my experiences of interviewing, getting to know, and writing articles about them.

Because it is a memoir of those happenings and not an autobiography of my entire life, personal subjects and family members are mentioned only in relation to such events.

But since they are mentioned here and there throughout the book, I will fill in just a few facts about them here.

My beloved husband, Robert Franklin "Bob" Ames originated and operated *Four Wheeler Magazine*, as well as *Western Treasures, and Car Classics,* for several years. He was considered an authority on the subject of four-wheel-drive vehicles and off-road driving. In addition, he wrote and published several books, including the *Gold Prospector's Handbook*, which he authored under the pseudonym Jack Black, and which is still in print and even more popular today. He was always there for me, enabling me to carry on my own career. And he passed on all too soon in 1988,the result of a brain tumor.

I was left with our two grownup sons, David and Jeffrey, and now have two grandsons, Garrett and Nicholas, whom Bob never lived to see.

Ralph Merlino, my longtime photographer and friend, shared many of the adventures described in this book, so he is mentioned considerably.

Other than that, we rarely got together, and, since Ralph always supplied our transportation, picking me up at my place, I never even saw where he lived. Today, he has moved to a ranch in the state of Texas.

Of course, we also shared dozens of eaten-out lunches. About them, I can only say that it's a good thing I like tomatoes because whenever any appeared on the plate of tomato-hating Ralph, they eventually ended up on mine.

Chapter 1
Time Out(Doors) With Tippi

"Walk faster, Shirley. That elephant is going to run over you."

The callous amusement of my good friend and long-time photographer Ralph Merlino annoyed me. It was easy for him to talk. He was off to the side and of no special interest to the animal in question.

Me? I was directly in front of the humongous creature. And, in my hand, I carried the thing he wanted most in all the world at this moment – a tiny box of Chiclets chewing gum. I was learning that elephants can, indeed, pick up the pace when they have a good reason to.

"I'm going as fast as I can," I retorted. As I tried to increase my speed even more, I found myself stumbling over the uneven, rock-encrusted soil. The cowboy boots I was wearing were better suited to riding than walking – at least in places like Tippi Hedren's Shambala Preserve.

Shambala is Sanskrit for "a meeting place of peace and harmony for all beings, animal and human." So far as Tippi was concerned, it was this 180 acre stretch of stony, tree-and-brush-filled canyon north of Los Angeles, complete with fenced enclosures populated by some 70 lions, leopards, cougars, tigers and tigons (offspring of unplanned matings of tigers and lions) as well as two elephants and an assortment of birds and waterfowl. Most of the "cats" had been hand-raised by Tippi and her family, and their existence was largely responsible for the establishing of this place, which reminded me of the setting for the old *Daktari* TV series.

Tippi spent most of her daytimes here, caring for her animal friends and seeking ways to support their expensive taste for raw meat. To her, it was, no doubt, a sort of Paradise.

To me, at this moment, it was a scary place to be.

Although we'd been here before to do an article on how she dealt with the pros and cons of her outdoor life from a healthcare angle, today was different. We were concentrating on the animals up-close. So far, I'd been jostled by an oversized tigress who was trying to beat me through the gate of her private yard, where common sense told me I should never have been in the first place. And now this.

Moments before, with Tippi poling us across her private lake on a raft, I'd been fondly recalling my teenage visits to the old World Jungle Compound in Thousand Oaks, west of the San Fernando Valley. Lions and tigers and other animals trained for movie work had been housed there and were on display to the public. I'd enjoyed hanging out and patting the brillo-pad backs of water buffalos, posing for my picture with a smallish, blind tiger, and even dreaming of being rich enough to own an elephant some day. Shades of the Jungle Book stuff.

But, after today, forget it! All I wanted was out of here and away from Timbo or Kura or whoever it was sniffing down my neck!

Our purpose in Tippi's elephant area was for this mother of actress Melanie Griffith, and glamorous movie star in her own right, to demonstrate an interesting phenomenon – the passion displayed by this elephant for the items I held in my hand.

Fortunately, we had reached the spot she had chosen for the event.

Taking the package of gum, which I was only too eager to surrender, Tippi tossed a single tiny square into the cavernous mouth of her monstrous pet. Timbo (or it might have been Kura) caught it deftly, and, after a moment, assumed an expression of utter bliss. This continued throughout the entire package, which she gave him piece by piece with Ralph's camera snapping away.

It was hard to realize that this was the same lady who had portrayed a sophisticated, spoiled heiress mercilessly attacked by feathered, flying creatures in the 1963 Alfred Hitchcock thriller, *The Birds.*

Regarding that movie, she had told me, "Seventeen live, pecking gulls and ravens were tied to me in the attic scene, and afterward, I went to bed for four days, on doctor's orders – there, to fight off nightmares filled with flapping wings and bloody beaks."

Born Nathalie Hedren, to a Swedish father and German mother, in the state of Minnesota, she'd known dogs and cats and horses as a part of her everyday life. She received her nickname of Tippi from "Tupsa," a Swedish term of endearment used for her by her father.

She spent 10 years as a successful New York model before making a television commercial in California and catching the eye of Hitchcock. During the New York years, she married actor Peter Griffith and gave birth to her only child.

Later divorced, she married Noel Marshall, a TV commercials agent at that time, gaining three stepsons in the bargain.

While filming *Satan's Harvest* in Africa, Tippi found herself "overwhelmed" by her co-star, a magnificent animal named Dandylion. And, while touring through game preserves, the Marshalls witnessed an abandoned, flat-roofed Portuguese-style house which had been adopted by a pride of thirty lions.

Intrigued, they determined to make a movie based upon what they had seen. Since animals to portray the necessary parts proved to be scarce, they sought out cubs to hand-raise; hence their eventual acquisition of the land which became Shambala.

Chapter 2

Stars In My Life

One of my earliest memories is of my mother taking me to see a motion picture starring Jeanette MacDonald and Nelson Eddy that impressed me so much that, next day, when invited to sing a song in my Kindergarten class, I obliged with warbling "The Indian Love Call" in my five-year-old voice.

As a young girl in Des Moines, Iowa my favorite pastime was going to the movies with my second cousin, Joyce. For a good share of my life, she was my best friend.

Our mothers, Nina (pronounced to rhyme with Dinah) and Laureen, were first cousins and had also been best friends. Joyce and I had been born just 11 days apart and in the same hospital. However, she, the older, was a Taurus (born May 16) and I am a Gemini (born May 27).

In our younger years, with our vivid imaginations, we often pretended to be the characters from the motion pictures we had seen. But, since we both insisted on "being" the heroine, we had to stretch that role to accommodate two. We swung on a "jungle vine" rope, suspended from a tree to hold a wooden swing seat, to play double "Janes" after watching the *Tarzan* movies. As "cowgirls," we raced across the lawn on invisible horses. And, in our minds' eyes, we flirted with handsome leading men, who greatly admired the beautiful women we pretended to be.

Little did I know then that one day I would personally get to know many of the 1930s and 1940s era actors and actresses I so admired -- along with a lot of other latter-day famous motion picture and television stars and famous authors. Not only that, I would visit their homes, talk to them, write articles about them for publication in an assortment of magazines and newspapers, and occasionally have my picture taken in casual, friendly poses, with them. Some I would see more than once, over a period of years.

The first star we saw in person on moving to California in 1942 was spotted by my dad, Gene, on The Santa Monica pier – a place we frequented to purchase smoked fish to be eaten by hand with soda crackers. It was Arthur Lake who portrayed Dagwood Bumstead in the *Blondie* movies.

And sometime later, after he had become a real estate broker, Dad had occasion to meet John Carroll, a dark-haired, handsome, mustached hero of several movies I had seen. I, too, met him when I accompanied my father to a community meeting.

When I enrolled in 11th grade at Hollywood Professional Children's School at the age of sixteen, it wasn't to see stars; it was in order to be able to practice "figure-style" roller skating at the Hollywood Roller Bowl in the afternoons.

The school had been around for quite a while and its purpose was to educate children and teenagers who were professional actors, actresses, and entertainers. Located in an office-like building on Hollywood Boulevard, it had no grounds to speak of. It didn't need any. School hours were from 9 a.m. to 1 p.m., with no recess, no physical education, and no lunchtime. School grades ranged from kindergarten to 12th grade, and class sizes could go from 10 to 20 attendees.

A main attraction of this private school was that students had the on-going opportunity to take temporary leave when necessary to fulfill a professional obligation. On returning, they were legally required to "make up time" by spending a designated number of extra study hours in a Study Hall style classroom.

My parents and I were living in the San Fernando Valley west of Los Angeles. I had spent some months practicing a roller skating spinning act with a young man named Philip Fox. It was an act based entirely on our double spinning, with me – as a "flyer" – being spun about by him in various lift positions. Centrifugal force was the secret of our success with this process.

Eventually, we gave up and broke up and I began taking freestyle roller skating lessons at the Hollywood Roller Bowl. I had thoughts of becoming a professional freestyle skater and joining a roller skating show. But, though I was a naturally graceful skater, participated in several roller rink shows and won medals in the American Roller Skating Association (ARSA) competitions, I really wasn't good enough. I could never get beyond the most basic spins and jumps no matter how hard I tried. And I did have most weekday afternoons to practice, thanks to the schedule of the school.

About three-quarters of my classmates were professional actors and entertainers of one sort or another. A number of assorted boys were members of a singing group known as the Mitchell Boys Choir. And. though I didn't exactly keep track of my classmates, following my high school graduation, I eventually noticed a few of their grownup accomplishments. Classmate Jody Lawrence, for one, starred in a popular movie named *Ten Tall Men*, opposite Burt Lancaster. And Classmate Larry Kert was to co-star with Carol Lawrence in the original Broadway version of *Westside Story*.

The school's alumni included Actor/Dancer/Singer Donald O'Connor — a favorite of mine. He never paid a visit to the school while I was there, but I was finally to meet him some 30 years later.

Donald and his wife were living in the hills above the eastern San Fernando Valley when my photographer-partner Ralph and I paid a brief visit for an interview and pictures, on a cover-story assignment for *Mature American* magazine.

Don and I walked around out on his patio to admire the view, and reminisced about our mutual "alma mater."

Some months later, when the Northridge earthquake occurred, I read that the O'Connor home had been damaged. Following that, they moved to Sedona, Arizona, red-rock country not known for earthquakes.

Chapter 3

More Stars and a Writing Job

When my uncle Charlie, along with his wife, my mother's sister Ruth, and their daughter, my younger cousin Jill, moved to California, he opened a one-man bakery in the San Fernando Valley town of Northridge. His only employees were my mother, my aunt Ruth, and me. Both my mother and aunt served as clerks, filling cases and waiting on customers.

Having helped with some of the baking in his former Des Moines bakery as a pre-teenager, I became his part-time baking assistant — frying doughnuts, mixing batches of white and chocolate cake (which I weighed on the scales in layer pans and baked in quantity), mixing frostings, and icing cakes. Eventually, my job also included some basic cake decorating. And, of course, when my mother and aunt were unavailable, I also filled in at waiting on customers.

Next door to the bakery was a cocktail bar owned by Louis Ameche, brother to one of my earlier movie heroes, Don Ameche, who specialized in musicals. If Don ever visited the bar, we never managed to see him. However, Louis became a regular customer of ours every time he "went on the wagon." On those days, he would stock up on selections of my uncle's delicious Danish.

Directly across Reseda Boulevard was a gift shop owned and operated by tall, blond Actress Nancy Kulp, best known for portraying Jane Hathaway, assistant to "Mr. Drysdale" on *The Beverly Hillbillies* television series. Her, we did see from time to time.

Another favorite of mine had always been the exotic (India) Indian actor, Sabu, who began his career as the young star of the 1942 movie version of *Jungle Book*. My mother had informed me that he was an occasional customer.

One day when both of us were working at the bakery, I came from the back to place fresh cakes in their proper case. Not wanting to interfere with her work as she bagged rolls and cookies for a person I took to be a dark-skinned woman wearing a turban, I tended strictly to business.

When the customer departed, Mom turned to me and asked, "Did you see him?'

"See who?" I queried.

She gave me a look of disgust. "Why, Sabu, of course."

And, though we never encountered the by then wheelchair-bound famous actor Lionel Barrymore, he, too, was a regular customer, frequently sending his man servant to purchase an assortment of "goodies."

But perhaps most impressive was our once-a-year privilege of providing the birthday cake for Desi Arnaz, who lived within easy driving distance with his wife, Lucille Ball.

The cake order was always the same, but "Lucy," who came in to order it herself, could never quite remember what kind it would be so had to be reminded. The answer? A banana-and- whipped-cream-filled sheet cake fashioned to resemble a guitar.

It was my uncle Charlie who got me started as a "selling" professional writer. An enthusiastic reader of the then international daily newspaper, *The Christian Science Monitor*, he suggested I submit personal experience essays to its Youth Section part of the Family Features page.

Soon, I was a regular contributor, with topics such as sleeping in the backyard on hot summer nights, picking raspberries on a trip to Washington State, riding horseback in the local mountains, working at the bakery, and any other experiences I could put into words. And I earned paychecks, of $2.75 and $3.50.

Although my full name at that time was Shirley Lee Brown, I decided to use just Shirley Lee as my "writing name," anticipating that I might one day be dealing with a married name, but would always be Shirley Lee. (I have lived to regret that move as there are more people named Shirley Lee than I had supposed. Let me also say that I was definitely not named for Shirley Temple who was not yet well known by the time I was born. Instead, my mother chose my combination name after seeing it in a coat label.)

Sometime later, I visited a local weekly newspaper nicknamed the Pink Sheet for its colorful front page, with sample clippings in hand, and was hired as part-time features writer and proof reader.

Among people I interviewed were actor/dancer Dan Dailey, who was Master of Fox Hounds to the Valley Hunt Club. Society editor Margaret Cronk , a member of that organization, arranged for me to visit him at his home and do an article for the paper.

Winding up a country lane, distinguished by a residents-only guarded gate, I found his house sprawled across the last hill on the road.

Dan was friendly and showed me around, including a brief

visit to see the fox hounds. Since their kennels and runs had not yet been cleaned for the day, I was glad to keep that part of my interview brief.

I also met my future husband, Robert Franklin "Bob" Ames, while working at the paper. The foreman of the "back" shop, where the paper was physically created, he was also a successful freelance writer with credits that included a couple of auto club magazines.

Soon, he was teaching me the ropes so that I, too, (aside from my part-time job) began to sell larger, more impressive articles, including personality profiles based on interviews and "travel" stories featuring interesting attractions. This was helped by Bob's outstanding photography as he accompanied me on several occasions.

Among other topics, I wrote about a well known cowboy performer named Montie Montana, for a *Christian Science Monitor* article that earned him an invitation to put on a show in England. Years later, he became famous for appearing annually in the Pasadena Rose Parade.

Other topics included Travel Town in the Los Angeles Griffith Park. For that one, which appeared in *National Motorist* magazine, we took along Bob's young niece and nephew to photograph among the retired trains.

However, it wasn't until a few years into our marriage, when we were already the parents of our two sons, Bob had founded and was operating *Four Wheeler Magazine* and I was selling fiction stories to *Teen Magazine*, that I began the celebrity writer route in earnest.

Chapter 4

Again and Again with Glenn

Glenn Ford was one of my very first celebrity interviews. It was 1972 and , I'd picked up a book on the bargain counter of a local bookstore entitled *Glenn Ford, R.F.D. Beverly Hills.*

I'd been a fan of his for as long as I could remember and I very much enjoyed this book, written by him about his experiences of gardening. Originally intending to cajole his only child, Peter, into eating vegetables Glenn decided to grow some vegetables at home in Beverly Hills. Because he said that he believed in "gardening with love," I thought the *Christian Science Monitor* would like an article on the subject. I queried, they accepted, and I set about requesting an interview.

Since Glenn was starring in the *Cade County* TV series in those days, I went through the CBS network to make my request. A phone call came within a few days, to inform me that I might interview him on the set at the studio.

We met on the shadowy soundstage, and talked sporadically between takes. I was taken by his soft, gentle voice, which I recognized immediately from the many movies of his that I'd seen. Of necessity, since we were constantly interrupted, I asked if I could quote from his book to help expand the article and he willingly agreed. When the story appeared in the *Monitor*, I sent him a copy and received a gracious handwritten note of thanks in reply.

This was only the beginning of what turned out to be a more than 20 year professional relationship.

One interesting thing I was to learn about his background was that, being of Welsh descent, he was born Gwyllyn Samuel Newton Ford in Quebec, Canada, in 1916. He later took his professional name from Glenford, the town that was the site of his family's paper mill and the scene of his early childhood. He was still a youngster when he accompanied his parents on their move to Santa Monica, California, where he received his education and gained his letter in track and baseball.

Glenn earned his spending money in some interesting ways in those days. He sold newspapers, cleaned up at the neighborhood pharmacy and café, operated the searchlight on the roof of the Wilshire Theatre on vaudeville weekends, and served as a stable boy for Will Rogers, who taught him to ride and to play polo.

On one of my visits to Glenn's house, he told me a story to illustrate what he thought of as a misrepresentation of his old friend and mentor.

"We were sitting around the living room of Will's ranch house one day after a polo game, and a newspaper man was there," he began.

"In the article that man wrote, he reported Will Rogers as saying, 'I never met a man I didn't like.' That saying became famous all over the world, but those aren't exactly the words that Will really said." Glenn paused for emphasis.

"I was seated right next to him at the time and what he actually said was, 'I never met a man *who liked horses* that I didn't like.'"

I found out a lot more about Glenn's love for plants the first time I visited the long-term Beverly Hills home he'd designed for himself. Situated on an approximate acre of hillside land, on a street in the neighborhood of the world famous Beverly Hills Hotel, the 14 room split-level house had a two-story tall atrium with an indoor sprinkler. An 18 foot tall Kentia palm was flanked by philodendrons bordering the indoor staircase.

His patio contained both flowers and vegetables. Roses and flowering shrubs around the pool gave way to redwood tubs of lettuce, carrots, tomatoes, herbs, and other delicacies. He preferred growing strawberries to a lawn of grass, and grapes to decorative vines. And there were about 150 fruit trees about the property, including orange, lemon, lime, apple, pear, peach, plum, apricot, fig, avocado, nectarine, tangerine, guava, persimmon, and kumquat. On top of his guest house was an orangery, patterned after gardens in Versailles.

"I'll match my corn-on-the-cob with anybody's," he proclaimed proudly. "I'm the original Beverly Hillbilly. I tried raising chickens, but some people must have complained, because the police came to see me and explained that it just wouldn't do. I'm sure my neighbor, Dinah Shore, wouldn't object to hearing roosters crowing, but there are others who don't appreciate being awakened early. I think the police were afraid that the next thing I'd do was get a cow."

Not content with growing food, he'd spent two sessions at the Cordon Bleu Cooking School in France, and collected recipes from around the world.

He told me of the difficult time he'd had acquiring the recipe for chicken livers from the chef at the Pump Room of the Ambassador Hotel in Chicago.

"He never wanted to tell me the secret of how they were done. But one day he decided to put together a book of celebrities who ate there, with their favorite Pump Room recipe. I struck a bargain – my picture and recommendation for his chicken liver secret. It's simple. You soak them overnight in a bowl of milk, which actually turns brown from the impurities it sucks out of them. Then I like to sauté mine with ginger and maple sugar. Delicious!"

On one occasion, I was on assignment to *Coronet* magazine and was expecting to meet Glenn's brash young publicist, Jay Bernstein, at the house. I'd arrived on time, but Jay failed to show.

I enjoyed a delightful interview with Glenn, circling the walls of his den and hallways, which were covered with autographed photos, framed mottoes, and words of wisdom of everyone from President Carter to Albert Schweitzer. There were awards and notices of appreciation from such groups as the Boy Scouts of America, Blind Babies Foundation, and United Jewish Appeal.

I learned that his personal talents included painting and sculpting, and that he loved to fish and hunt.

He'd enlisted in the U.S. Marine Corps in 1942 and, later, spent two years of active duty with the III Marine Amphibious Force in 1968 and '69. He was a Captain in the United States Naval Reserve at that time and had the distinction of being the only actor to serve with the Green Berets Special Forces. The medals he wore in such movies as *Midway* were really his own.

"When I made the war movie *So Ends Our Night* in 1941, Hitler's propaganda minister had put my name on a list of actors they wanted to take prisoner to make examples of them if they ever went into the service," he told me. Luckily, he was never captured.

After that war, Glenn had occasion to visit Hitler's bunker. "It was just a mound of earth, but they left a hole that you could enter by, so I went down and walked around. I found that I knew it pretty well from having read about it and seen the map of how it was laid out." His consensus was that Hitler did, indeed, commit suicide.

We spent a leisurely couple of hours together that day and I was just being escorted to the door when Jay arrived. Glenn and I exchanged a grin, acknowledging quietly to each other that we felt like a couple of kids out of school, having conversed on our own without the benefit of censure.

As usual, I received a note of thanks for my efforts when the ensuing article appeared..

By the time I accepted an assignment to do an article on Glenn for *Girl Talk* magazine, he had a new wife and a new publicist.

"I happen to adore women," he'd once said to me. "I think they are the greatest creatures God ever made. I like being around them. There's no such thing as an ugly woman. I've worked with some of the most beautiful and attractive women in the world." Indeed, his first wife and the mother of his son was the lovely actress/dancer Eleanor Powell.

Meeting his third wife, Cynthia, I found her likeable and interesting. The long-haired young woman was a Wilhelmina model. She was into photography, stained glass painting, and needlepoint, as well as being a working actress.

I included Cynthia in my article about Glenn, and, when it appeared, sent a copy to Glenn, as usual. Almost immediately, I received the following, beautifully handwritten, note: "Dear Shirley, Thank you for sending Cynthia and I the copy of the article in *Talk Magazine*….It was without a doubt, the nicest story ever written about me and I want you to know how much I appreciated it. With respect and love, Glenn Ford. P.S. If I had my way, any story written about me would be done by you."

I was elated until, just a couple of days later, I had occasion to call his publicist to request another interview for a different publication.

Feeling utterly optimistic about my expected reception, I was shocked when he told me sternly, "Shirley, don't count on it. I don't think Glenn will *ever* work with you again. You didn't get him the cover on that last story."

"But," I sputtered helplessly. "I never promised him the cover. *Girl Talk* doesn't put men on its cover."

If that were true, I wondered, why had Glenn written me his wonderful letter? Did he simply consider it common courtesy, but didn't really mean it?

Heartbroken, I did a very unprofessional thing. I sat down and wrote Glenn a letter in my own – unbeautiful – handwriting, telling him I was sorry if he had expected a cover story, but that I had, indeed, made no such promises.

It was a Friday afternoon when I sent it, feeling I had done all I could to make amends.

On Sunday evening, Bob and the boys and I were sitting down to dinner when the doorbell rang. There stood a Western Union person who presented us with a telegram to Shirley Lee.

The message was brief. "Shirley," it read, "Call me right away. My telephone number is _____. Glenn Ford."

For the next forty-five minutes – while my dinner grew cold – I spoke with both Glenn and Cynthia. Glenn told me that he didn't care a bit about being on the cover of a magazine – he'd been on so many over the years. He said that Cynthia's mother had seen the article in the magazine at her beauty parlor and had called to talk about and it and how pleased they had all been.

"From now on," he concluded kindly, "Don't go through anyone else to request an interview with me. You have my number. Just call me personally at home."

And from then on – over the course of many varied articles and many years, I always did.

Chapter 5

A Way To the Stars

In the late 1970s, I queried a national magazine located in the East called *In the Know* about an article idea I had. Upon receiving an answer to the effect that that magazine and another well known one called *Coronet* had been purchased by a publisher only blocks from my home, I quickly paid a visit to their office. Before long, I had become a regular contributor to those publications, working on assignment with both of their editors.

I became acquainted with a public relations lady named Harriet Modler, who was working for Television Producers Sid and Marty Krofft. With her help in suggesting ideas and arranging meetings, I was soon doing articles on the Kroffts, themselves, as well as some of the actors appearing in their productions. They included Mary Wickes, young Johnny Whitaker, Billy Barty, and The Osmonds, to name a few.

Brothers Sid and Marty Krofft were the super talented producers of a batch of children's television shows including *H.R. Pufnstuf*, *Bugaloos*, and *Lidsville*, as well as *The Donny and Marie Osmond Special* and its resulting series.

But prior to that, they had been famous for their 1962 *Le Pou-*

pees de Paris, the first "topless" Las Vegas style marionette show, which proved to be a hit at the Seattle World's Fair. In 1967, they had opened their own puppet theatre at Six Flags Over Georgia Park.

My first contact with the Kroffts and with Harriet had to do with my request for an interview with the young actress, Kathy Coleman, for a children's magazine. I was doing fiction and articles for a number of such publications, and I had become fascinated by *Land of the Lost*, a rather corny, but imaginative and entertaining Saturday morning kids' show, which was to become the inspiration for the 2009 movie of the same name.

My first personal contact with Sid and Marty came when Harriett persuaded me to do an article about their latest project – the creation of *The World of Sid and Marty Krofft* – the first indoor, high-rise entertainment park, which was planned to open in Atlanta, Georgia.

Bob went along on my interview to photograph some of the weirdest assortment of amusement park ride props we had ever seen.

Seated in their office, we learned some interesting facts about the pair. Their background stemmed from 200 years of puppeteering. The family's first puppet theatre opened in Athens, Greece in the late 18th century. Sid had been born in that city. As a boy serving his apprenticeship with his parents, he traveled throughout the world.

"When I was seven years old, I traveled all over, working as a puppeteer. I thought, 'What is my father doing to me?' but I've put everything I ever learned to use in some way," Sid told me.

Marty was born when the family was in Montreal, Canada. They were in London when the teenaged Sid was discovered by Jack Benny, who brought him to Hollywood to appear on a TV show. Later, his puppets became a regular feature of Judy Garland's and Tony Martin's nightclub acts.

"We always had one live person in our act, hidden among the puppets," he continued. "It would be a 'little person' – a midget or dwarf – in costume with strings just like the rest. Once there was a Frankenstein's monster puppet that cut his own strings. People thought he was operated by remote control. When they got backstage, they saw a puppet just like him and thought it was him.

"That was when we learned that people love to be a part of what they are being entertained by. Two-thirds of the show was what came after the stage performance. We explained the puppets to them and their eyes lit up with interest. This didn't distract them from the wonder; it added to it. They came back again and again, but we never let on about the 'live puppets.'"

When Bob and I toured the factory, we could see that all of Sid's projects were imaginative ones. And his fabulous creations were being constructed by some 175 industrious workers. Former salesman Marty's talent lay in handling the practical part of the business.

One of the wildest things being worked on at that time was the Pinball Machine Ride. Four people could fit into one of the eight-foot-high silver and black polished balls -- which were equipped with individual sound effect microphones -- and go whirling across a surface of bumpers, flippers, bells and scoring holes, while Goliath-sized coins wobbled about. The park entrance was planned to lie between two 18-foot-tall mimes riding upon a 47-ton, three-level crystalline carousel that would float on a cushion of air. The visitor could choose as his mount any one of 55 fantastic mythological creatures of the sea, land, or air, delicately rendered in glisteningly lovely transparent plastic.

Sid's eyes twinkled with enthusiasm as he paused to admire the handiwork of his crew. "Aren't they beautiful?" he asked, lovingly stroking a graceful 800-pound centaur and seating himself inside a sculptured seashell. Further along on our tour, a 3000 pound plastic whale rested, with open mouth inviting passengers.

My article on this subject appeared in the May, 1976 issue of *In The Know*.

Chapter 6
Fun with the Osmonds

It was only a couple of months later that my cover story on Donny and Marie appeared in *In the Know*.

I had met with the kids in one of the offices at the Hollywood studio being used by the Kroffts, and immediately noted the following about them, which I used near the beginning of my article:

To be a member of the Osmond family is to belong to an exclusive mutual admiration society. Ask Marie who's her favorite performer of all. The answer? "Donny." Ask the same of Donny and you'll get "Marie." But, persisting, after that, who? For both of them: "Jimmy Osmond." And, as a last resort, seeking someone beyond the clan: "The Osmond Brothers." You'll get a few good-natured giggles along with the answers, but the sincerity is not to be mistaken.

However, I quickly learned that the Osmonds not only liked each other; they liked *everybody*. "You can find something to like about everyone," insisted Marie. "If you don't like someone, it's because there's something the matter with *you*."

At a mere 16 years of age, she was working hard with her part of "carrying the show." Her schedule included four hours a day with her private tutor. Donny was taking college courses and favored electronics.

Father George and mother Olive Osmond spent lots of time on the set of the show as well. At that time, only four family members remained at home on their cattle ranch in northern Utah. While the show was in production, those involved shared quarters in a privately owned apartment building in the Los Angeles area where even Marie had her own individual apartment.

"I've heard so much about your purple socks," I said to Donny. "Tell me what it's all about, please."

"That was the color of my first bicycle and it's my favorite color," he replied with a grin.

"My mom and I decided to give him a gag gift of 30 pairs of purple socks," added Marie.

"So after that I said that all my socks would be purple from then on," finished Donny.

To date, he only had one of the original pairs left.

Although our interview had been fairly short, it was not to be the end of my Osmond family associations.

Because I also was a contributor to the children's magazine, *Jack and Jill*, which was running a series featuring kids talking about unusual family connections and occupations, I proposed an article to be entitled *My Family Is the Osmonds*, which I would write as an as-told-to with 13-year-old Jimmy Osmond.

Told through the eyes of the youngest Osmond brother, a lot of details came to light. I'll let Jimmy's words fill in a few more of them here:

"I was born in the town of Canoga Park, in the San Fernando Valley area of Los Angeles, California. When I was two years old, I taught myself to swim in the family pool. My family had lived in the state of Utah before I was born, and we all moved back there when I was still pretty young…..Five of my brothers are married and they have made me an uncle nine times….My sister Marie is an extra special pal of mine. She takes me Christmas shopping and she sticks up for me. We even had the chicken pox together, which Dad says is a great way to share things. Of course, it was Donny who gave it to us. Donny and Marie both have cars that were given to them for doing a car commercial, so they both take me around, and, sometimes the three of us go to the movies together. I saw *Jaws* four times."

Jimmy had things to tell about each of his brothers. He said that he and Donny were roommates in their Los Angeles area apartment building. And he admitted to playing a trick on Donny by putting a dead crab under his pillow. Alan, Wayne, Merrill and Jay were the four original members of the Osmond Brothers barbershop quartet. Wayne, he said, was the pilot of the family, and Jay the choreographer. Merrill was Jimmy's "look-alike" brother, his "twin."

He told of going to private school at home and studying by mail with the American School, on the set. Math, he claimed as his 'favorite subject.'

"For several years, we went to Japan, and I appeared in a soft drink commercial in which I spoke Japanese. I didn't exactly learn the language, just the sound of the words, so I could say what they wanted me to. I also earned the family's first gold record for a song I sang in Japanese."

Jimmy ended by saying "I'm proud of all my brothers and of my sister, too, and I really enjoy working with them."

I decided to suggest doing an article on the mother of the

brood, which I was to call *The Unsung Osmond*. Given the go-ahead, by my editor, I visited the set of the show to spend a couple of hours with Olive where we sat in the audience section of the theater.

A more mature version of Marie, with dark hair, brown eyes, and a charming smile, Olive had been born in Samaria, Idaho to school teacher parents of the Mormon religion. During the school year, the family lived in town; then spent the summer on their wheat ranch, where she delighted in driving a tractor. Her only sibling – a brother – was 10 years her junior. During high school, she played saxophone with her school band and for Saturday night dances.

Following a crash course in business and typing, she did her patriotic duty by going to work for the War Department in Ogden, Utah, where she eventually met the young Army sergeant who would become her husband.

Olive instilled the love of music in the couple's eight boys and one girl. She taught them to read music and encouraged them to play a variety of musical instruments. It was their father, George, who taught them harmony. It became their custom to put on regular weekly performances for their grandparents and at church programs. Their first big break was being "discovered" by Andy Williams' father during an engagement at Disneyland. Olive herself appeared several times with the family on *The Andy Williams Show*.

Olive explained that her two older sons, Virl and Tom, did not perform with the family, due to hearing disabilities. Instead, they lived in Provo with their families, and took care of the family's many business matters and promotions.

Chapter 7

Big Little Billy Barty

One of my favorite people was the biggest Little Person I ever knew – or knew of. Actor Billy Barty might have been a mere three feet, nine inches tall, but his heart, his dreams, his talents, and his accomplishments were beyond measuring.

Although Billy had appeared in more than 200 motion pictures, on hundreds of television shows and on stage in theaters and nightclubs all over the world, show business was but one phase of his busy life.

In 1957, he organized the Little People of America to help the more than a million citizens under four feet, 10 inches in height. In 1975 he started the Billy Barty Foundation for related projects. And – in 1994, which was the last time I had the pleasure of writing about him (for *Mature American* magazine) -- he hosted the 22nd annual Billy Barty International Invitational Golf Tournament. At the time of that writing, he was also serving on the Los Angeles City and County Commission Disability Programs.

Every time I had reason to visit Billy – at his home or his office – I was made to feel like a friend. But his home was the most fun. There, I would also have the added enjoyment of talking with his wife, Shirley, another Little Person, somewhat taller than Billy, at four foot, three inches.

The couple, along with their two children, lived in an average looking house on a quiet, tree-lined side street. But, inside, it had been altered to better suit its inhabitants. In the kitchen, the sink, stove, and counters had all been lowered to fit the lady of the house. And, though most of the furniture was regular size, the bathroom showers and closet racks were also low. Billy's home office furniture accommodated its owner's size; while the family cars – though full-size vehicles – had extensions added to the gas and brake pedals.

Billy had been born into a family of average size people in Millsboro, Pennsylvania. Happily, he was never made to feel different. If he couldn't reach something, he was told to climb up on a chair. He began his show business career at the tender age of three, after his family moved to California. He explained that it happened due to an unusual stunt he developed – spinning upside down like a top.

"My dad was carrying me in his arms down the sidewalk in front of Selznick Studios. They were filming outside, so Dad put me down and said, 'Billy, do a head spin for the director.' So I stood on my head and spun around and the director saw it and put me in a movie."

His early movies include *Alice In Wonderland, A Midsummer Night's Dream, Gold Diggers of 1933, Footlight Parade*, and the *Mickey McGuire* comedies of Mickey Rooney, who became a life-long friend. At the time of my final interview, his most recent films included *The Day of the Locust, Firepower, W.C. Fields and Me, Under the Rainbow, Foul Play, Masters of the Universe, Tough Guys, Willow*, and *Life Stinks.*

While traveling the vaudeville circuit with his two average-sized sisters, at about the age of eight, Billy met another special friend – Donald O'Connor. Many years later, the two worked together at the London Palladium. After graduating from a professional children's school, Billy majored in journalism at Los Angeles City College. Despite his diminutive size, he participated and lettered in football there and in basketball at Los Angeles State College (now Cal State, L.A.). He also served as Sports Editor and public relations director for athletics there. Although he considered a career as a newspaper reporter for the *Hollywood Citizen-News*, show business proved more appealing.

Billy excelled in television. His performances were widely varied – from featured appearances with Steve Allen and Milton Berle and dramatic roles on shows such as *Playhouse 90, G.E. Theatre,* and *Alfred Hitchcock Presents* to Saturday morning kids' show roles like Sparky the Firefly on *The Bugaloos* and *Sigmund and the Sea Monsters.* As a sea monster, he struggled with a scratchy foam rubber costume weighing 15 pounds. I was told that he could only stand it for 15 minutes at a time.

In 1953, he joined Spike Jones and his band as a performer and spent eight years touring the United States, Canada and Australia. He then went to Europe to appear in his one-man show. In 1960, he hosted *Billy Barty's Big Show*, which ran for four years on Metromedia Television, predecessor to the Fox Network. He also guest-starred in a number of sitcoms.

Although Billy never minded telling jokes about his size, he was a staunch and serious champion for everyone suffering from any of the many forms of dwarfism., and he did his best to help them with physical, mental, and social problems. Though he was among those who preferred the term Little People (with the accent on little), he was quick to say "There's nothing wrong with the word *dwarf*. It simply means short."

When the couple's daughter, Lori Ellen, also a Little Person, four feet tall, was twelve-years-old (in 1976), I wrote an article entitled *My Father Is Billy Barty*, with her, for *Jack and Jill Magazine*. In that story, she mentioned her brother, Braden, then only five-years-old, whom she explained would "grow up to be taller than average." She was right. By the time he was a teenager, he was more than six foot tall.

Billy's matter-of-fact attitude toward life is revealed in the following incident, which he related to me:

It seemed he had been asked to help out with an eight-year-old boy whose physical growth seemed arrested at three feet, five inches. The youngster had been spending his school days kicking and spitting at his classmates. Billy rushed to oblige.

"At the principal's request, I went out to talk to the whole school, but I insisted upon talking with the child (we'll call him John) first.

"I said, 'Hey, John, how come you're kicking and spitting at the kids?'

"He said, 'Because they're calling me short.'

"So I said, 'You *are* short!"

"The kid did a double take. He wasn't expecting me to say that.

"So I said, 'You're a Little Person, like me. Next time someone says you're short, say, 'Yes, I'm short. I'm just like Billy Barty.'"

Chapter 8

Two Teen Stars — Johnny Whitaker and Valerie Bertinelli

Johnny Whitaker

Because young Johnny Whitaker had been co-starring with Billy Barty in *Sigmund and the Sea Monsters* – one of the Krofft's Saturday morning kids' shows about two brothers who discovered a sea monster named Sigmund near their beach home and made friends with him – it seemed like a good idea for me to interview him for a children's' magazine. I contacted the editor of *Young World*, a sister publication to *Jack and Jill*, which aimed for a slightly older crowd. (The article appeared as a cover story in the January, 1977 issue.)

At the time when I visited the Whitakers' sprawling, tree-shaded, two-story home in the north part of the San Fernando Valley, Johnny was in his late teens – about two years older than my eldest son, David. We started our tour in the large, well-lighted kitchen, which Johnny's mom referred to as 'Grand Central Station,' because so much seemed to be going on there all the time. I found Johnny to be friendly, talkative, and unassuming as he led me up the stairs to view the bedroom he shared with his younger brother, Billy.

"I recently redecorated it in red, white and blue, with a nautical theme," he said proudly. "I caught that fish in Florida." He indicated a mounted, 24-pound barracuda. On another wall was a framed set of Apollo patches said to have been transported to the moon, which he told me had been presented to him on his thirteenth birthday.

Johnny was born in Van Nuys, California and had seven brothers and sisters. He began his professional career with a TV commercial at the age of three, and was a mere six-years-old when he started to play Jody, the twin boy in the original version of the television series *Family Affair*, with Brian Keith, Sebastian Cabot, and Anissa Jones, who portrayed the girl twin, Buffy. The series had run for six years.

After that, Johnny had had important roles in four Disney movies, *The Biscuit Eater, Napoleon and Samantha, Snowball Express, and Mystery in Dracula's Castle.*

Jodie Foster co-starred with Johnny in *Tom Sawyer,* a movie musical production based on Mark Twain's famous story. He'd been considered a "natural" for that part due to his curly orange hair, freckles, and cheerful grin.

"My whole family went along on location to Missouri," he said. "They all dressed up in costumes as extras in the movie."

Johnny had many interests. He went to a public high school much of the time and enjoyed acting in their amateur productions. He'd served as Yell King, during their football season, and he was active in Boy Scouts. He swam in the family pool, helped to barbecue, and liked cooking breakfast for his family. And he enjoyed growing vegetables in his family's back yard.

He could speak both Spanish and French. But I was most impressed by his "talking" the sign language of the deaf, which he'd "picked up" through charitable work for the John Tracy Clinic for deaf and mute children and from a book on the subject.

He told me of two incidents when his knowledge of that skill proved useful. One day when two girls were talking sign language across the classroom, he surprised them by joining in their conversation. Another time, he found himself seated next to a deaf woman on a cross country plane flight. He was able to assist her in communicating with the stewardess, much to the woman's delight; then enjoyed a long conversation with her.

Johnny was raised in a family that was community oriented. During disastrous brush fires that swept through the mountains above their home one November, they helped to evacuate and feed neighboring fire victims.

Beside continuing his acting career, Johnny was to become president of Candlelight Enterprises, a computer consultant firm based in Hollywood, and also created an Import/Export business.

Valerie Bertinelli

Valerie Bertinelli was a cute 15year-old young lady when first I met her. But she was already quite an accomplished actress. I'd enjoyed watching her on the *One Day at a Time* television series in which she co-starred with Bonnie Franklin and Mackenzie Phillips.

Her personal manager, Tami Lynn, arranged for us to meet at her own tree-shaded San Fernando Valley home.

"Hi," said Valerie, when I walked through the door.

"Hi yourself," I said back.

I'd already learned a few things from the bio I'd been given.

Valerie had been born in Wilmington, Delaware, and moved to southern California with her parents and four brothers in 1971. She enrolled in the Tami Lynn Academy of Artists in Sherman Oaks and decided to turn "pro." Before landing her role as Barbie Cooper, she'd appeared in several television commercials, United Way service announcements and the series *Apple's Way.*

"How do you like working on television?" I asked.

"It's fun," she answered, "and I love my TV mom, Bonnie Franklin. But I have to put in three hours doing schoolwork with a tutor every day so they have to shoot around me. .When I can I'd rather attend my own public high school. I'm a cheerleader there."

For fun, she said that she liked to ski, play tennis, swim in the family pool, and go horseback riding with her friend, Kathy Coleman, co-star of the Saturday morning kids' show, *Land of the Lost."*

Unlike your average high school girl, she had her own new Camaro, which she was driving with a learner's permit, and was also hoping to take flying lessons someday.

About her career, she told me, "I'm working hard to be good enough to do all sorts of parts, including musical ones. I'm taking singing, dancing, and piano lessons. "

After my story was published in an issue of *In The Know,* I was surprised to receive a phone call from Valerie's father.

"I just want to thank you for writing such a nice article about my daughter," he said.

It was a few years later that I had occasion to interview her again for *Young Miss* magazine. We met at the Metromedia offices in Hollywood and it was fun to talk with the more mature young lady and reminisce about our first meeting.

Chapter 9

Totie and Karen and Dick, Oh My!

Dick Van Dyke

Dick Van Dyke was actually the first person I interviewed exclusively for *Coronet* magazine.

Checking *TV Guide* for ideas, I ran across the announcement that Dick Van Dyke would be having a variety series called *Van Dyke and Company*. Aha, I thought. A good story idea and a chance to meet a man whose movies and TV shows I had always enjoyed.

We met in his dressing room at the Burbank studio of NBC before going to lunch. Dick did a brief little soft shoe routine as I sat there watching, enthralled.

When we sat down, along with his PR man, at a private table in the busy commissary, I told him that my editor wanted him to talk about his recovery from alcoholism and he graciously obliged.

"Five years ago, when I was 45, I decided to retire because I thought that 'old age' had robbed me of my vim, vigor and vitality," he said heartily. "My family and I moved to a ranch in Arizona and I prepared to sit back and watch the world go by. But then I discovered that the real reason for my inertia was alcoholism and that total abstinence would be my fountain of youth.

"I feel reborn," he exclaimed enthusiastically..

In fact, for two seasons, he'd taped *The New Dick Van Dyke Show*, a sit-com, at Carefree, Arizona, with another season in Hollywood.

Since they did not care for the pressures of living in Los Angeles, the Van Dykes had moved to a house on the bay in San Diego, where they enjoyed owning a 33-foot sloop. At this time, they were also maintaining the Arizona ranch with a caretaker, and visiting there during cooler weather.

During the taping of this new show, Dick was living in a rented house not far from the NBC studios, "batching it" throughout the week. On Fridays he made the 20 minute flight to San Diego for a couple of days of home life and sailing.

The time had come for his two o'clock call for rehearsal.

Returning to the subject of alcoholism, he said, "It's what happens after you've conquered the thing, and it's all over, that's truly amazing. You feel completely different. You see so many new things to do. It's really a sort of spiritual awakening."

As he walked off down the hall, I could hear him singing to himself.

Totie Fields

My interview with the remarkable comedienne Totie Fields came just six weeks after she had begun walking with a prostheses following the amputation of her left leg due to diabetes. It was to be a lesson in optimism.

Waiting in the cheerful green and white living room of her Los Angeles area high-rise apartment, I was startled to hear, "I'm here."

Totie – who had just returned from having her hair done in preparation for her first photo session standing and walking on her artificial leg for my article -- made an impressive entrance. Her svelte new figure was attired in a smart black pinstripe pantsuit and she carried a slim black and silver cane with a bird's head handle.

"I'm dying to get back to work," she told me. "With my new leg, I feel totally whole. I was told I would. I knew I *never* would. But the truth of the matter is that they were right and I was wrong."

Earlier, Totie had received the coveted Las Vegas Entertainment Award for the Female Comedy Star of the Year.

"Handicapped does not mean losing a limb," she offered. "Not being able to enjoy a day, whether the sun is out or isn't, or not being able to enjoy trees and flowers is handicapped. Today, I drove by a bed of pink and yellow poppies and I went out of my mind. We turned the corner and parked to look. And when a poppy makes you excited, I think it's a wonderful day."

Totie began her professional career as a band singer at the age of 14 while still attending high school in her native Hartford, Connecticut. It soon became evident that she had an innate ability to make people laugh. Her comic mind was inventive, agile and quick.

At 18, she moved to Boston. While appearing at the Frolics Club, she met George Johnston, who was the comic on the bill. He not only fell in love with her wit; he fell in love with Totie. The two were married and, under her husband's tutelage, she learned the fine and difficult art of the professional comedienne. Later, she was doing Standing Room Only nightclub engagements from Las Vegas to Miami, and had starred on virtually every TV variety show.

She told me that when Ed Sullivan saw her show at the Copa, he hated her, but his wife Sylvia loved her. "I was put on *The Ed Sul-*

livan Show as a dare. He said, 'I'll show you, she's going to bomb.' But I was a hit and I ended up doing more than 30 of his shows."

Karen Grassle

Although television viewers had come to think of her as the meek and proper pioneer wife and mother of three little girls on her long running series, "*Little House on the Prairie,* I learned that she was really quite different. (Her last name is pronounced grass' lee.)

Sweet, gentle, and soft-spoken, she was. Meek, she was not. At the time that I visited her Hollywood Hills home, she was deeply engrossed in being a spokesperson for battered wives.

Karen had been a champion of women's causes since early childhood. When a school project centered around a telescope that was to be built from a kit, she gave a speech, saying that she thought a girl should be allowed on that committee. She won that reward for herself. I noted that there was an expensive looking telescope of her own standing beside a large view window.

Karen's high school days were spent in Ventura, California. Her professional career had included the study of ballet and jazz dancing, theatre arts (and an English major) at the University of California in Berkeley, and a Fullbright Scholarship which enabled her to study for a year at the London Academy of Music and Dramatic Arts, where she later worked as a teacher. She appeared in repertory theater throughout the country and on Broadway, and created roles in three daytime television programs: *Love of Life, Love Is a Many Splendored Thing,* and *The Guiding Light*. A film brought her back to California, where she was offered the part in *Little House on the Prairie,* opposite Michael Landon.

Chapter 10
Getting In the Swing

By this time I was getting into the swing of celebrity interviews. I had some regular markets for my articles and I had learned that many of the well known people I interviewed liked my work and would make themselves available to me whenever I offered them an article in a publication of which they approved. Some actually agreed to appear in one of the so-called tabloids since the articles I wrote for them were of general interest and never stressful gossip. And, though they were one of the better paying markets, I never went against any person's wishes if they chose not to be in them.

Failure to produce and/or to please were generally no problem once I had a legitimate assignment. But there were exceptions.

When one of the teenage magazines I wrote for expressed an interest in the Jackson family singers (they were known as The Jackson Five in those days) I contacted their agent by phone and received an invitation to meet with them at their San Fernando Valley ranch house.

I drove to their street, parked, and met that gentleman at the gate of the property. We walked toward one of the doors to the sprawling establishment where we were eventually met by one young man.

"Where is everybody, Tito?" queried the agent anxiously. "Shirley has an appointment to meet with all the family for an article interview."

The total quiet of the place warned us that things were not as they should be.

Tito shook his head. "I don't know. They all went off somewhere but they didn't tell me or take me with them."

So that was the end of that project. No notice to their agent and no apology coming.

On another day, I met Robert Hegyes, better known at that time as Juan Epstein in the *Welcome Back, Kotter* TV series, at a Hollywood restaurant. We enjoyed a pleasant hour or two and I wrote up my assigned article for a young people's publication.

As agreed upon, I mailed him a copy before sending it in to the editor. My purpose was for an accuracy check, but, otherwise it was a polite exception to what most writers thought of as an unwritten rule: Don't show your article to the person interviewed .before publication.

I had considered Hegyes to be a wholesome and talented young fellow and had done my best to make him interesting to my teenage audience. I knew acceptance of the article was a given. But I had not reckoned on the actor himself.

"I don't want you to print it," he told me vehemently over the phone. You made me sound too boring and innocent!"

Short of accusing him of drug use, alcoholism, or some sort of crime, I didn't know what changes I could make that would please him, and, if I did so, the magazine would have no interest in the article anyway. So again, I had hit a dead end.

An interview with David Groh, the ruggedly handsome actor who portrayed Rhoda's husband on the series of that name was more successful, if brief. Likewise one with handsome young black actor Ron Glass, who played Detective Sergeant Harris on ABC-TV's *Barney Miller* series.

And Geri Jewell proved to be a "gem" of an interview. I sold several articles to various publications on the cheerful young actress-comedienne, who, though afflicted with cerebral palsy, was a "semi-regular" on the TV series *Facts of Life* at that time.

She told me a bit about her background. Mistakenly pronounced dead at birth, she was a premature baby weighing only three pounds. She spent her first three months in an incubator, survived a bout with pneumonia, and was found to have cerebral palsy – a disorder of the nervous system (caused by her traumatic birth) that made it impossible for her to fully control her muscle movements. Other results of her condition were a speech defect and hearing loss.

Although doctors did not expect her to be able to walk, her mother worked with her to make it possible. By the time I met her, she not only walked with a limp, she could drive a car, ride a bike, roller skate, swim and even play a mild game of football.

From the age of 12, Geri had wanted to become an actress-comedienne like Carol Burnett. She eventually became a hit in Los Angeles Comedy Stores, impressed Norman Lear while performing at a benefit dinner, and was given her chance on *Facts of Life*.

Another young actress I interviewed at this stage of my career was Melissa Sue Anderson, who was portraying Mary Ingalls on the *Little House on the Prairie* TV series.

She was seventeen when I met with her on her day off -- immediately after she had returned from a stint in the rugged hill country of northern California -- and she had been playing that role since the age of eleven.

"While we were on location this time I did all my own stunts, so I'm covered with scrapes and bruises," she told me. "It was great fun, but I don't think they knew how physically difficult some of the scenes would be or they might have hired a stuntwoman for me.

"I was supposed to be lost and trying to get help for a wrecked stagecoach. Since I'm playing the part of a girl who is now blind -- and hadn't even a cane to help me -- when the land sloped, I would fall and roll all the way down the hill. The first time I did it, I fell right on my face."

She said that one scene called for glasses she was carrying to fall from her pocket and magnify the sun to start a fire, which had been set for that purpose.

"I was back against some rocks and the heat was terrible. I had been told to wait there as long as possible before moving away, but the wind changed and the flames got closer and closer. I heard someone shout, 'Get out of there,' and I tried to run, but it was difficult in my long skirts. My hair was close to being singed and I really thought I might already be on fire. Somebody dashed down and grabbed me and pulled me out. I was certainly glad when it was all over." She paused. "It was exciting though."

Melissa told me that she had read the *Little House on the Prairie* book and others in the children's series by Laura Ingalls Wilder (which actually started with the one entitled *Little House in the Big Woods*) when she was eight years old, but, of course, had never dreamed that only three years later, she'd be "living" a part in the story for a television audience.

I recalled that I, too, had enjoyed those books as a little girl, but I remembered that my mother had brought them home from the Des Moines public library and read them to me.

Chapter 11

Radar Leads To Hollywood Squares

Do you recall Gary Burghoff, better known as Radar of the *M*A*S*H* television series?

His request to me for being interviewed was that I follow him around on his day off to observe and photograph his many varied activities.

The result was that Bob and our sons and I went to the home Gary shared with his wife, Janet, and toddler daughter, Gena, in what I chose to describe as "idyllic park-like surroundings in a secluded area of Malibu where huge sprawling sycamores and giant, frothy ferns abound."

The day had been planned to include a tour and pictures of the property, showing Gary's backyard food fish tank, an 18-foot Doughboy above-ground pool, which he had stocked with trout and catfish. It was one of the ideas he proposed to alleviate any sort of food shortage.

Next came an excursion to a private tennis court to watch and photograph his weekly tennis lesson. He paused in mid-serve when the hum of an airplane was heard overhead, then laughed and apologized. Referring to his television series, which was being shot on location, he explained, "I stop living when a plane goes over. On the set of the show, it ruins the shot, so we just have to give up and wait it out. It holds over even into my private life. When I'm in the pool with my wife, I even stop swimming."

Another reference to the show was his explanation that, although he had no reason to wear glasses in real life, he had decided his character should wear them to explain why he should have such acute hearing that he was aware of the helicopters coming before anyone else.

We ended the day with Gary by meeting him at the NBC Studios in Burbank, to watch and photograph him on what you would call now the original *Hollywood Squares*.

We were allowed to bring David and Jeffrey along, and, once the show began, sat in very uncomfortable, but privileged, canvas VIP seats at the front of the studio. Since two episodes were being shot that evening, one after another, we trouped up to the overflowing buffet table with the others during the mid-time break.

That evening prompted me to seek an assignment with *In The Know* magazine for a story about *Hollywood Squares*.

This time, my interviews were with producer Jay Redack, co-contestant coordinator Ida Mae McKenzie, announcer Ken Williams, host Peter Marshall, and a few of the stars in their dressing rooms.

I was to begin my article thus: "What's seventeen feet tall, made of tubular steel and plywood, has orange colored lights, and holds nine celebrities at a time?" The answer, of course, was the giant 'tic-tac-toe board' used for the show. Before going home that night, I was allowed to climb aboard the none-too-steady structure and experience it for myself.

Other show facts I learned were that the premise had been officially copied in London, in Amsterdam, and in Australia under such names as *Butter, Eggs and Cheese* and *Naughts and Crosses.* It took four to five writers perusing newspapers, magazines and books, to produce the 20 to 30 questions – ranging from anthropology to safety tips, homemaking and Hollywood gossip – that were needed for a single half-hour show. During its over 10-year run, up to that time, more than 100,000 questions had been used. And, in the stacks of letters received by show officials, there had been many stating that lives had actually been saved through information garnered from the show regarding tornadoes, fires, and other disasters.

I also learned that it took 30 people, including electricians, just to set up the board, not to mention those who chose the contestants. It took at least six men to move the giant board from its "permanent home" in the NBC hallway through the "elephant doors" and into place in the studio. And it was said that most of the stars agreed that the giant prop's nickname was "Shaky."

When I dropped in on Comedienne Joan Rivers, who was resting in her dressing room with her young daughter, Melissa, she told me how much she enjoyed the show, saying she never missed watching it at home if she could help it.

"You learn so much," she insisted. "I'm always passing on these odd bits of information to my husband. Of course, he couldn't care less, but it really impresses me."

I also had occasion to visit briefly with the tall, handsome, "spooky" actor Vincent Price. "I credit ninety percent of the show's success to its host, Peter Marshall," he told me. "He's generous and warm and he never plays down or puts down anybody."

Since, at that time, five days of programming were shot in one day with breaks for "lunch," the host and his stars arrived at the studio with five changes of clothing.

Ida Mae Mackenzie explained that contestants were chosen for their "energy and vitality" and for "smiling and competing," as well as being the kind of people that others at home like to watch." They were generally given two auditions and a written exam. One in a hundred was selected to go on the show and 16 were needed on "stand by" for each taping.

This sixtyish lady considered herself an excellent judge of people and "other things." She had many stories to tell, but my favorite was the one about a very pregnant contestant who showed up, insisting that she had "two weeks yet to go" before her baby was due.

"I took one look and said, 'Honey, I think it's going to be much sooner than that. You go on home for this time and come back after you've had the baby.'" With a big grin, she gave her punch line. "The baby was born that very night."

And, yes, the new mother did return to go on the show.

As for me, direct results of my doing the article were interviews and subsequently published articles with Paul Lynde – a center square favorite, Peter Marshall, and Betty White.

Chapter 12

I Interview a "Silly" Man

I was nervous about meeting with actor/comedian Paul Lynde, even though I'd had no trouble setting up an interview. The reason was that *People* magazine had touted him as bitter about being typecast as "the man in the box," in reference to his popularity in that cherished center position on *Hollywood Squares*.

I was to be pleasantly surprised.

Arriving late, as I'd become confused by a similarity of winding street names in his Hollywood Hills neighborhood, I was shocked to see a For Sale sign on his property. My dismay was due partly to the fact that the house had been suggested to me as a possible topic for conversation.

I soon found out that the door I entered on arriving there was a virtual "tip of the iceberg." It was merely the top floor and entrance hallway of a luxurious five-level, hillside estate. We promptly descended to the lower floor living room to conduct our interview.

My pleasant surprise came when I learned that not only Paul, but his female publicist, who was also present, was a Gemini like me. We all hit it off immediately. There seems to be something about people with my Sun Sign that links us together, even though, of course, I should and do deny that I truly take those things seriously.

The sale sign in front of the house was explained thus by Paul:

"I only stayed here as long as I did because of my dog, Harry, since he was old and blind and needed to know his way around. I had to have him put to sleep last August. I want to live in New York where I'll have an apartment and commute to work in Hollywood.

"I'm moving into a flat-level house in Beverly Hills that's half the size of this one so I can simply lock the door and leave. It isn't that I don't like California. No one could dislike the climate here. It's simply that I *love* New York. I'm more creative there. There's night life there and I'm a night person. Most of my good friends live there, too. Here, my friends are 60 miles from me and in New York, they're five minutes away."

I was relieved to find that Paul was unhappy with *People* magazine's interpretation of his relationship with *Hollywood Squares*.

"Although I've been quoted as saying I hate *Hollywood Squares*, that's very far from the truth. It's been the greatest thing in my career. When I started out the first year, I would not be a regular. I was frightened of it, because I'm really a 'script man.' Now, after ten solid years, I know what I'm doing. It became easier each time I did it."

He explained that his reason for wanting to "ease out" of the show was that he wanted to do more movies and not become typecast as strictly a television performer.

"I really want to be a movie star," he admitted.

Paul's eleven movies up to that time included *Bye Bye Birdie*, *Under the Yum Yum Tree*, *Send Me No Flowers*, *Gidget Grows Up*, and the cartoon feature *Charlotte's Web*.

He told me about the enormous amount of fan mail he received via *Hollywood Squares,* mentioning that some of the letters were especially interesting and touching.

"A great many parents of retarded children write and tell me that I am the only person to whom their child reacts. They say that their children have fantastic senses of humor and that I turn them on."

A regular contributor to The Retarded Children's Foundation, he said he loved children both individually and collectively and expressed an empathy for their particular problems of getting along in the world.

As a child himself, he admitted to living in a world of fantasy whenever he was allowed to. One of a family of six, he developed a weight problem at an early age, due to a lengthy illness, and said he felt "lost in the shuffle."

"I lied a lot as a child," he said. "I had an Aunt Nettie, who was sort of like 'Auntie Mame.' Her children were grown and I loved to go to her house. She would indulge me in every lie I told. My own mother was too busy with five other children and a house to care for to give me the time and enjoy me. She had to disapprove of my lying. My aunt would give her whole day to me and just let me lie to her all day long."

Having been "born wanting to be rich and famous," Paul, at five years of age, spent lots of time sitting on the front steps of the local Mt. Vernon mansion, waving at passing cars.

His dreams came true eventually, but with lots of effort on his part. He majored in theatre arts at Northwestern University, then went to New York, where he managed to survive with financial aid from his father. But tragedy entered his life with the death of his mother and his father in the same year.

He earned his living in a variety of ways that included waiter, hotel clerk, ambulance driver, and even a blood donor before his big break came when he was signed for *New Faces of 1952* by Leonard Stillman. Nine years later came the "turning point" with his starring Broadway role in *Bye Bye Birdie*, which he later reprised for the movie version.

I loved talking with Paul, who told me that his favorite word was "silly." He didn't want to just be funny; it was "silly" that most appealed to him.

I was to end my *Coronet* article on him with the following quotation, which referred to the fact that he was not going to replace his dog, because he wanted to commute between Los Angeles and New York. "I couldn't do that with a dog. I wouldn't put a dog through it, and I wouldn't leave a dog for a week or even a half a week at a time. So I'll wait until I really retire. Then I'll live in a kennel. I want a dog of every kind."

Unfortunately, Paul Lynde did not live to retire. I visited him once again in his "flat land" home, but he died of a heart attack not long after moving there.

Chapter 13

At Home with Peter Marshall

I arrived at Peter Marshall's wooded, hillside home in the San Fernando Valley just as workmen were preparing to pour a new driveway. Reminiscent of a Swiss chateau, the house was attractively rustic, with heavy shake shingles, used brick, and wood that I was to learn had been treated for weathering. Shade trees, plants, a view, and a swimming pool, on a lower level of the property, lent further interest.

Peter appeared, casually clad in a gray sweatshirt and blue jeans, and led me through a side door into the pleasant, two-level kitchen. Up close, I was duly impressed by his six-foot, three-inch height – which towered over my five-foot, two-inch self – as well as his smiling, dark-haired comeliness.

While he made tea for us, he explained that he'd been reconstructing this once small, older home for over a year, turning it into a larger, more unusual one. He'd replaced floors, added authentic saloon doors from a pub in London, a New England stained glass church window, and a large second-story bedroom-office wing with a balcony, marble bath and a six-foot advent television screen hidden away behind a wall made from a former barn door.

From Huntington, West Virginia, he said that he was raised on both coasts.

"I love the San Fernando Valley and I looked for a year and a half to find this place. I wanted a house to re-do and finally settled on this one."

After being given "the grand tour," I settled down with Peter to talk about other things, but, largely, about *Hollywood Squares*.

Since the show's beginning, in 1966, there had been well over 2,000 segments to date at this time (1977), with Peter hosting every one of them, never missing for any reason.

He remarked that he cared about the outcome of the game in regard to the contestants he tried so hard to put at ease.

"I try to be neutral," he explained, "but I feel terrible when someone goes away without even winning $200. It's depressing. Still, the parting gifts are always worth at least three or four hundred dollars – and they've had the opportunity to be on television"

He admitted to having made a mistake during one segment.

"One night I inadvertently gave the answer to a question myself. I had asked a question of Roddy McDowall and he couldn't think of a bluff. It was getting late and I was getting the speed-up sign, so I said, 'Well, the next question, Roddy. What is the country of Gaul known as today?' And he said, 'France.' I said, '*That's right!*'

"Everybody looked at me for about five seconds, realizing what I'd done. It was so dumb! And the contestant said, 'I agree with *him*!' So we had to throw that question out. But, thank the Lord, the guy got the next question right."

Besides *Hollywood Squares*, Peter was, at the same time, involved with *The Peter Marshall Variety Show*, featuring a wide selection of celebrity guest stars that had included Leslie Uggams, Charo, John Davidson, Valerie Bertinelli, Donny Most, and Alice

Ghostly, to name a few. He was also making personal appearances at Las Vegas, Reno, Tahoe, and Dearborn.

Divorced, Peter was the father of two daughters and two sons, all grown up. At this stage of his life, he was living alone, doing his own washing and cooking, with the help of a part-time housekeeper for cleaning jobs

Born Pierre La Cock, he'd changed his name for the stage. His sister, Actress Joanne Dru, had also tried the surname of Marshall for a time. Peter began his career as an NBC page in New York City, but was soon working in plays both on and off Broadway. He starred on Broadway with Julie Harris in *Skyscraper*, and played the lead in the London company of *Bye Bye Birdie*. Teaming in a comedy act with Tommy Noonan, he appeared in leading nightclubs, on *The Ed Sullivan Show*, and other TV variety shows. He starred in two motion pictures – *Ensign Pulver* and *The Cavern,* and cut several records. In 1974, he made his Las Vegas stage debut as the opening act for Marty Allen's show and earned rave reviews. And, in 1973-74, he won two Emmy Awards – Daytime Host of the Year and Best Host of a Game Show, Daytime Programming.

Peter's personal interests included writing and spectator sports. "That's why I have that TV set-up in my bedroom," he told me. "It's fantastic for sports."

But he was also particularly interested in acquiring unusual antiques. "I'm into country furniture – French, English and American." Some of his favorite acquisitions included an Amish rocking chair, an American saw buck table, a library ladder-chair (which he used as a planter) a 1780 grocery counter from Vermont, which he planned to use for a bar), and an authentic playbill featuring Tyrone Powers' great-grandfather.

Chapter 14

Gale Storm: The Once-Upon-A-Time Girl

"Once upon a time there was a lovely young girl who won a talent contest and, subsequently, the prepared name of Gale Storm, met a handsome young man who was her male counterpart, fell madly in love, got married, became a successful actress, and lived happily ever after."

So began the article I wrote about Gale Storm for the April, 1977 issue of *Coronet*. All of that was true (except for "happily ever after, since her first husband, Lee Bonnell was to pass on in 1986 and Gale was to follow him in 2009). They had been married for 35 years and were the parents of three grownup boys and a teenage daughter at the time of my first visit to her home.

By then, Gale's most famous television series', *My Little Margie* and *The Gale Storm Show, Oh Susanna*, were being seen only in reruns. But the vivacious star was every bit as cute and bubbly as ever, even though she was a grandmother three times over.

We sat in her spacious living room, with its slate floor, Palos Verde rock fireplace, green and orange accents, and wide picture windows looking out on a backyard patio, swimming pool, shade trees and shrubs and a teahouse on the slope above. This single-story ranch type house was located on a hillside on the southern edge of the San Fernando Valley.

Gale told me this story, which prompted the above-mentioned opening to my article:

"I was born Josephine Owaissa Cottle, the youngest of five children, in Bloomington, Texas. We moved to Houston while I was still quite young."

She paused to tell me she'd been told that her middle name was Native American for "bluebird."

"When I was in high school, I entered the local *Gateway to Hollywood* contest," she continued. "I won the female half, so the next step was to go to Hollywood, where young men and women from all over the country were gathered to compete in the finals.

"When I walked into the room where we were to meet the others, I took one look at the tall, handsome young man standing by the piano and I knew that was it! Later, I went straight to the room my mother had rented next to the Studio Club, where the girls were housed, and told her I had just met the man I was going to marry.

"This wasn't like me. I'd always been a sensible girl and had expected to remain single for a good long while in order to bring comforts to my mother, who had taken in sewing in order to raise her five children after my father died when I was still a baby.

"Others tried to discourage me by saying that Lee wasn't for me and I would only get hurt. They might have hoped to get him for themselves. I thanked them for their concern, but I paid no attention. I felt that God had intended we should find each other and, before many weeks had gone by, so did he."

Officials of the contest, wanting to help her, even though the other actresses didn't, linked her with Lee Bonnell whenever possible, even pairing them for a bride and groom skit. But at first, he compared her to his younger sister.

"In the skit, I had to say 'I love you' to him and I just couldn't seem to get it right." She grinned wickedly, reminiscent of her Margie character. "He was concerned about it, so he spent lots of time coaching me in the part. By the time we finally did the skit, he was saying it to *me*, and meaning it!"

Both turned out to be contest winners, with the result that they would become known professionally as Gale Storm and Terry Belmont, and were put under contract to RKP Studios.

"I had been so worried that Lee would win and I would lose. If that had happened, my mother would have taken me home to Texas and I wouldn't get to be around him," she admitted.

In a little over a year, the two were married.

Gale was put to work right away in the *Tom Brown's School Days* film. She also entered the RKO Schoolroom with Roddy McDowall, Jimmy Lydon and some others.

After appearing in a wide variety of motion picture roles, Gale moved on to her television career. as well as a singing career that resulted in the selling of over 6,000,000 records and a gold record for her first rock and roll sensation, "I Hear You Knockin'".

Not quite so successful, Lee eventually settled for a career in the insurance business.

Gale and I had a continuing professional relationship for quite some time after that. One evening, she and Lee also entertained my husband, sons, and father (who was a widower, following the death of my mother in 1971) and me in their home. My dad, long a Gale Storm fan, was delighted by the opportunity to meet her.

Then, in 1990, taking Ralph along, I met with Gale once more for a *Whatever Happened To…* magazine article. By that time, following Lee's death, she was living in a Los Angeles apartment, having married a former ABC executive who had been introduced to her by mutual friends. We enjoyed reminiscing and she told me a story regarding the gargally sound known as 'the Margie gurgle,' which she made when caught off guard and found guilty of some minor discretion.

"My daughter, Susanna was born in 1956 during the making of my *Oh Susana* series. When I'd play with her, I'd make that noise to her and she would make it back to me on cue. I told my director about her and he decided to write her into an episode, with me babysitting for a friend.

"I thought he was crazy because he had me sing her to sleep. I thought 'she's gonna lie there and never go to sleep.' She was in a bassinet where she could pull herself up. She'd sit up and I'd push her back down and sing to her. And he was right. She not only did 'the Margie gurgle"; she went to sleep on cue."

Chapter 15

My Betty White Connection

My long-time association with Betty White began with the *Coronet* cover story I did on her for the May, 1977 issue.

The *Mary Tyler Moore* television show was calling it quits, after a four year run, and Betty would no longer be playing the role of Sue Ann Nivens, whom she referred to as "the neighborhood nymphomaniac."

We met at the studio during her lunch break and were driven by limousine to a nearby restaurant where we both ordered mushroom omelets.

Over this pleasant meal, I learned a lot about some of the things Betty and I had in common -- we were both "only" children of our parents and had enjoyed happy, companionable childhoods with our moms and dads.

"I've heard that you and Mary Tyler Moore were friends before you joined the cast of the show," I remarked. 'Did that help you to get the role?"

"It almost prevented it," she answered with a chuckle. "They said they wanted 'a Betty White type,' but felt that our friendship might create an awkward situation. But after they tried a few other people, they decided to give me a chance."

Betty was an active member of the Board of Trustees of the Greater Los Angeles Zoo Association, the Morris Animal Foundation, and the American Humane Society. She had written, edited, and produced a special called *Backstage at the Zoo*, and had a television series called *Pet Set*, featuring celebrities and their pets. That very evening, she was scheduled to go on *The Dinah Shore Show* with Jill and Evelyn – a baby orangutan and a baby gorilla. At home, she had three dogs at that time.

"I've always enjoyed playing games," said Betty, "and that's how I met my husband." (By this time, she'd been married to Allen Ludden for 14 years and had helped to raise her stepchildren, David, Martha and Sarah.)

"Allen and I actually met on *Password*. We did one week of shows. I liked him very much, but that was it. Then we got booked into the summer theatre productions of *Critic's Choice*, playing opposite each other. We both thought it sounded like a good idea. Allen's wife had died and it was the first summer that the kids were without a mother. So he bundled them all up – and two poodle puppies – and he brought them to Cape Cod. I got to really know the whole family and we all became very good friends." Betty and Allen were married the following year.

"When I was a teenager, I watched you on the local TV show with Al Jarvis," I told her.

"We were on every week day for five hours," she recalled. "It was live television in those days and you had to learn to cope with anything that came up. The commercial people would bring in their copy for a two-minute commercial. You'd get a quick look at it, then go out and do the product. I'd glance at the copy and then ad-lib it. It usually worked.

"We had Doctor Ross Dog Food for that show and then Kermin's Frozen Pies. Well, this one time, they got the jingle going for Doctor Ross and then they turned the light on the frozen pies. It broke me up and I laughed so hard that we ended up losing both accounts."

Betty took over that show after two hosts moved on to other projects and did it all by herself for a total of 30 hours weekly. Later, she formed her own production company and produced and starred in *Life With Elizabeth* and others.

Our meeting was far too brief, but I was pleased when Betty sent me a very nice letter after my article was published, thanking me for "the beautiful cover story" and especially for my "accurate quotes."

It was to be the first of several letters she sent to me over the next several years, which, unfortunately, were gentle refusals of my requests for interviews for various publications.

So, it was a pleasant surprise for me, when, in 1994 – long after I'd begun working with Ralph Merlino – that we clicked on my assignment for a *Mature American* cover story.

When we arrived at her home, Betty greeted me like an old friend.

Her Cape Cod style house was surrounded by an acre of manicured lawns, boasted a backyard hilltop view, a large swimming pool, and a wide variety of colorful flowerbeds. Inside, we found examples of Betty's own needlepoint, a large collection of Steuben glass, and five Emmys, one of them Allen's.

Although Allen passed away in 1981, and the human kids were grown and off on their own, Betty still had plenty of "family" around. Besides a live-in housekeeper, there were both cats and dogs, which she allowed to sleep on her bed at night.

A lot had happened since we'd been together. She'd completed seven years with *The Golden Girls*, a one-season spin-off, *The Golden Palace*, and a series with Bob Newhart called *Bob*, among many other projects.

She was currently writing a book about her early days in television. And she already had three published books to her credit, including one called *The Leading Lady, Dinah's Story*. It was written in partnership with Tom Sullivan, the well known blind singer, songwriter, lecturer and author of his autobiography, *If You could See What I Hear*, which was made into a 1982 movie. The book he wrote with Betty dealt with the dual life of a seeing-eye dog that spent nine years guiding Tom, and on her retirement, went on, for several years until her death to become a loving companion to Betty.

Mentioning her attendance at a retrospective meeting at the Museum of Broadcasting in New York the previous Fall, Betty said she had encountered an old friend there.

"It was Jane Wyatt, known for her long-running television series *Father Knows Best*.

"She and I were forever being mistaken for each other in the old days. At the meeting, they showed some clips of our early shows and it was incredible how much we resembled each other. Back then, I'd go somewhere and people would say, "Oh, Jane Wyatt, how nice to see you." She'd go somewhere and they'd say, 'Hey, Betty.'

"Jane told me that even on vacation, she'd run into the same problem. Once she and her husband went fishing and stopped for coffee in a very little town in Maine. When the man came to take their order, he said, 'My gosh, it's Betty White.'"

Chapter 16

My Collector Angle Starts with Elke

Just when I thought things were going well with my celebrity writing career, the publisher who had purchased *In the Know* and *Coronet* decided to close down those two magazines.

It was around this time that I joined The American Society of Journalists & Authors, which was based in New York City, with chapters across the country – the nearest to me being in Los Angeles. In those days, we writers (and our spouses) held dinner meetings in the old Los Angeles Press Club adobe building. To reach our meeting place, we climbed a narrow stairway to a room crowded with a long table and accompanying chairs. The food we were served was not great. In fact, we joked about trying to identify the main course of the menu, but it was all great fun. Networking meant sharing tips about magazines and editors willing to hand out assignments.

This connection led me to join The Hollywood Women's Press Club and for many years, as a member, I helped to stage their annual Golden Apple (celebrity) Luncheon.

I decided to branch out and try to find some new markets. On reading about a publication of The Franklin Mint, called *The Franklin Mint Almanac*, I wrote a letter to the editor, explaining that my teenage son, David, was a member of an adult coin club and had been since the age of eleven. Would they be interested in having me write about some of the West Valley Coin Club's many distinguished members? I asked.

I was amazed when I received a reply that what they really wanted were articles about celebrities and the things they liked to collect. To date, they'd run stories about Joseph Cotton, Irving Stone, Charles Addams, and Joan Fontaine, among others. They said if I had access to people like that, I should contact them again.

Before I had time to give much thought to this new concept, I answered a phone call from an editor there, requesting that I take over an assignment that had already been set up. It was to drive to Beverly Hills and interview Actress Elke Sommer about her pewter collection. The photographer had already been assigned.

All I knew about Elke at this time was that she was a beautiful, short-haired blond from Germany who'd co-starred with Paul Newman and Edward G. Robinson in a movie I had greatly enjoyed called *The Prize*.

I followed a curving drive up a hill to the secluded house above a tennis court, noticing the two iron dogs that flanked her front door. When I rang the bell, several live dog voices answered; five of which appeared to greet me when the door was opened by their owner.

Elke led me through a large hallway and into a rustic living room featuring a high ceiling with yellow-painted beams and two huge beige leather couches sharing a door-sized coffee table. Straight ahead, an antique merry-go-round horse, stripped to its native wood color, served as a newel post for a short stairway leading to a raised annex. At right angles to the couches, a unique gray-toned fireplace was enhanced by the dominant reds of large Chinese pictures. Religious figures and chubby angels completed what I could see of the décor.

Tall, rangy writer Joe Hyams, Elke's husband at the time, wandered in to say hello and depart.

"Turn around if you want to see pewter," he instructed me genially as he left.

I did, and there, sure enough, were the yellow painted floor-to-ceiling shelves full of it on either side of the doorway. Plates and pitchers, bowls, tureens, mugs, spoons, and other "trifles" with odd pieces interspersed. As my eyes became more discerning, I spotted many pewter items throughout the room…a pair of two-foot tall ornate candle holders, for instance.

"I like pewter because I use my pewter," Elke told me, relaxing on one of the couches. "Old silver is very nice, but I like more of a country feeling about the way I live. Pewter has a quality and texture to it which I'm crazy about. When I have a dinner party, I use the twelve tankards – the English ones – to drink wine out of. And I use the plates."

I learned that Elke was born in Berlin near the close of World War II, the only child of a Lutheran minister and his wife. They moved to the country after the war. Her father, who was descended from 13th century robber barons, died when she was only fourteen, and she worked as a mother's helper and "domestic" in London, to help finance her education as a language student, studying to be an interpreter. She was fluent in at least five languages. While in Italy on vacation, she'd won a dance contest and been "discovered" by an Italian movie producer, and had roles in movies made in Rome, Berlin, France, and England, before her first American one turned her into an important international star. In 1967, she'd been awarded the Silver Bambi in Germany as the Best Actress of 1966.Other of her movies had been *A Shot in the Dark* with Peter Sellers, and *Boy, Did I Get a Wrong Number*, with Bob Hope and Phyllis Diller.

It was quite by accident that she became a collector of pewter.

"I grew up in a village in Germany," she explained. "I'm a country girl really. I knew every calf and every cow. One time when I went back on a visit, I saw a dog drinking from what seemed to be a very nice bowl of a kind of grayish metal. I said to the farm woman, 'May I look at the bowl?' She said, 'Sure.' I recognized it to be an important German pewter, and offered to trade her an enamel bowl for it."

When the woman saw that Elke liked "that kind of stuff," she told her to check with the plumber next door because he was melting down all the old pieces and using it as welding pewter. (This had become a common practice following World War II, since there was nothing else available for mending metal cooking pots, water pipes and other items.)

Elke continued her story. "He's what?" I exclaimed in horror.

" 'He's already melted down a whole service of plates and cups and things,' she answered.

"So I ran over and grabbed hold of four or five pieces. One was a lovely tankard. I asked, 'Can I buy these things?' He said that I could if I would give him the price of welding pewter. So that's how I started."

Besides the collection in her American home, she said she had about 1500 pieces in her house in Germany. However, the ones she treasured most had disappeared, never to return.

"Very few people know that I'm actually a von," she said. "I have the title of Baroness, though I don't choose to use it. I feel that it's no merit to me. I simply inherited it. My ancestors had a castle, which is now in ruins due to bombing. From my aunt, I inherited about fifty pieces of the family pewter with my great-granddad's initials on them. I stored them in the dining room of the first house we owned in America, which later was determined by psychic experts to be haunted. After Joe and I decided to sell that house and move to a new one, a mysterious fire broke out in the dining room. My pewter melted down into nothing but little puddles on the dining room floor. The only thing left was the engraved center of a serving platter."

Elke said that it had taught her a lesson. "If a fire ever breaks out in this house," she insisted, "I will get all my pewter and throw it into the swimming pool."

Remarking on her unusual gray fireplace, I was told that she had wanted something to complement her pewter so she'd had it made of brushed steel.

While making my "pewter tour" through her home, I'd been attracted by colorful framed reproductions of some of her paintings. (The original, I learned, were off at an exhibition.) A self-taught artist, who was highly acclaimed by professional critics, she spent much of her time painting and sculpting and had also had her work reproduced on collector plates.

A few years later, I returned with Ralph to photograph and write about her artwork for *Collector's Mart* magazine. For the majority of her paintings, she drew on her childhood memories of events in the village of Niederndorf. Scenes depicted families enjoying such activities as boating, sleighing and skiing. They combined a childlike simplicity with an aura of sophistication. A special peculiarity was the fact that her people wore hats, but were barefoot.

"It's a thing with me," she said. "It means they are sheltered from above and very close to the ground. I like peasants with big feet and big hands, and I like something to be happening in my paintings. I try to put people in situations in which I'd like to find myself."

And how did she go about creating a design for a collector plate? I asked.

"To do that," she told me, "you have to think round!"

Chapter 17

More for Franklin Mint

Pay at the *The Franklin Mint Almanac* was reasonably good and I enjoyed the style of writing they insisted upon – well researched subjects with interesting people.

One of the next articles I did for them was divided into three sections. Under the title *Caught in the Act of Collecting*, it told the individual stories of three young actresses talking about their chosen collectibles. They were Jill Whelan, Barbi Benton, and Linda Purl. I visited all three girls in their homes.

Jill Whelan

It was fun meeting Jill Whelan, who portrayed the Captain's young teenage daughter on one of my favorite TV sitcoms – *The Love Boat*. An avid collector of *Gone With the Wind* memorabilia, she lived with her family, and a kitten-sized white Maltese puppy named Scarlett, in a quiet San Fernando Valley neighborhood.

Jill studied acting, singing, gymnastics and ballet while still in elementary school, then turned professional to work in television commercials. Her first motion picture was *Airplane* and her first TV series was entitled *Friends* (not related to the later popular series of the same name). As a regular on *The Love Boat*, she was spending most of her days between two soundstages, where the permanent sets were housed, or on cruises to locations like Mexico, Australia, and the Caribbean.

I was impressed with the knowledge this cute, fluffy-haired young girl possessed about her favorite subject.

She explained to me that her first encounter with *GWTW*, as it is fondly referred to by its many collectors, was via television. She was so entranced, that she read the novel, the biographies of its film stars, and as many other books as she could find about the picture itself.

Her collection included *GWTW* movie stills, posters, lobby cards, sheet music, Scarlett O'Hara dolls, and a boxed brick bearing the words "From Loew's Grand Theatre, Atlanta, Georgia, 1893-1978, World Premier Site of Gone With The Wind." (That theater burned down in 1978.)

When Olivia de Havilland (who portrayed the gentle Melanie) appeared on *Love Boat*, Jill picked up some anecdotes about the filming of *GWTW*.

"She told me about a joke she played on Clark Gable," Jill related with a laugh. "They were rehearsing a scene in which Rhett was to carry Melanie down the stairs. So Ms. de Havilland tied weights around her waist so that he couldn't lift her."

Barbi Benton

Of all the many famous people I have interviewed, the Pasadena area seven-acre estate occupied by Barbi Benton and her husband, George Gradow, was one of the most beautiful and impressive homes I had the pleasure of visiting.

I drove up a curving private road though stately redwoods, feathery palms, and flowering magnolias to the large parking lot of a wonderfully spacious, 15,000 square foot white 1930s era house.

I had become accustomed to a more frivolous side of Barbi, whose TV appearances ranged from *The Love Boat* to *The Tonight Show* and *Circus of the Stars*, a regular on *Hee Haw*, and the hostess of *Playboy After Dark*. I knew the pretty, long-haired brunette to be an actress, singer and nightclub entertainer. I did not know she had a vocal range of five octaves, had enjoyed seven international recording hits and captured the bronze award for America at the 1977 Tokyo Music Festival, was a pianist, composer of new-age music, and an experienced collector of art. Nor did I know she'd been a veterinary medicine student at UCLA, ran seven miles each day, raced with the U.S. Ski Team, and lifted weights in her own home gym.

My interview that day had to do with her hobby of collecting egg-shaped items of which she had more than a hundred, including such one-of-a-kind examples as a "deviled egg," sculpted for her by artist Charles Bragg, with a wicked looking demon emerging from the shell, and a bronze egg accompanied by three tiny workmen repairing it.

Linda Purl

Delicate blond Actress Linda Purl, who was born in Connecticut, has a special reason for her great interest in Oriental artworks. At the age of five, she had moved to Tokyo, along with her family, when her engineer father was transferred there.

She grew up speaking Japanese fluently, hosting and appearing on a National Education Network television program in that city for seven years as a child. The only American at that time to study at the famed Toho Gaino Academy, she acted in the National Theater of Japan's presentation of *The Miracle Worker*, and played the young English boy in *The King and I* (performed in Japanese), among numerous other productions.

Having returned to the United States in 1971, Linda's professional credits included eight feature films, 16 television films and two-mini-series. For a time, she had been married to Desi Arnaz, Jr., and they had remained friendly.

Because her parents were living in Hong Kong, she enjoyed shopping trips when visiting them there. Some of her collection items included a dipper from an Indonesian temple, Kabuki dancing fans, figurines, wooden dancer's masks, bowls, an abacus, and ornately carved wooden headboards.

Her Japanese garden, viewed through floor-to-ceiling living room windows, was created by a well-known architect and she employed a Japanese housekeeper, with whom she enjoyed conversing in the Japanese language.

Chapter 18

I Team Up with a Photographer

Freelance magazine article writers are inclined to hang out at magazine racks or shops to look for new markets for their work as well as for writers' magazines that include lists of the above.

My favorite hang-out at this time was a small news/magazine/book store on the corner of a prominent street in the San Fernando Valley community where I lived. Conversing with its owner, Ralph Merlino, and his wife, Nancy, I learned that he was a professional photographer who accepted assignments and sold his work to various publications, including the tabloids.

Although I didn't have a market for such a story, I agreed to meet him at the new Valley home of Kevin Tighe, who was then a co-star on the TV series. We spent a few hours there, but I was not able to locate a buyer for a story on Tighe at that time.

Nevertheless, Ralph and I agreed to work together if we could obtain a mutual assignment. A nice looking, dark-haired man. of medium height, ten-plus years younger than me, Ralph has a genial nature and loves to schmooze with his subjects. I was to find this both helpful and annoying, depending upon the situation, but I always appreciated his remarkable picture-taking talent.

About this time, I connected with the editor of *Collectibles Il-lustrated*, a magazine which was headquartered in the New England area of the country and was devoted to stories about collectibles and collectors of literally everything and anything,

Over the next three years (until it folded), this magazine would become a "mainstay" for Ralph and me as we traveled about southern California, producing stories and pictures about ordinary people who collected everything from tiny eye-wash cups, to full-size vintage gasoline pumps and antique diving helmets.

But what the editor really wanted most from us were the stories we supplied on celebrities who were collectors.

One of our earlier stories was a three-way combination one with Rose Marie, Richard Deacon, and Morey Amsterdam -- the trio of sidekicks on *The Dick Van Dyke Show.*, which had premiered in 1961 but was still being seen in reruns. All three were avid collectors of varied items.

Rose Marie

Rose Marie greeted us cheerfully in her San Fernando Valley home, of which she gave us a tour that included individual specimens of her collector plates and fine china. From kitchen and dining room to living room, hallways, bedrooms and even bathrooms, her collector plates covered walls, peeped out of drawers and cupboards and perched on top of shelves and tabletops.

Also popular *on Hollywood Squares*, she had been in show business since the age of three, when she was known as Baby Rose Marie, and had starred on Broadway, in movies, television and in leading nightclubs across the country. Her husband, Bobby Guy (first trumpeter for NBC's orchestra) was deceased by this time.

Rose Marie's collection had begun with some antique plates given to her by her mother but was now extensive enough to fill the walls of her home, featuring special items from all of her travels.

"Wherever I go, I try to find a plate that represents that place," she said.

The collection included service plates from various hotels in which she had stayed as well. There were many other special items, including collections of antique butter dishes and antique cups and saucers. And she had special dishes for holidays such as Christmas, Thanksgiving, and Valentine's Day.

Richard Deacon

Richard Deacon's collection of stone eggs prompted him to start our interview with a few chosen "egg remarks." And he wasn't too sensitive about the fact that his hair had receded toward the back of his head.

"Morey Amsterdam used to call me 'Egghead' when we were on *The Dick Van Dyke Show* together," he said amiably. "And someone made a cartoon of my head as an egg, which they used it as a dartboard on the show.

"My collection started because I enjoyed picking up shells on the beach," he told us. "Then I started going to mineral shows and began finding various minerals in polished egg shapes."

His items included rose quartz, malachite, jasper, moss-agate, ruby, Mexican opal, and both brown and blue tiger-eye. He also had a couple of real ostrich eggs and a pair of carved emu eggs.

Richard had appeared in some 50 motion pictures, a Broadway version of *Hello Dolly*, and on more than 30 television shows, including *Leave It to Beaver* and *The Beverly Hillbillies*.

He said that when he had duplicate "eggs," he might offer one to a friend who admired it, but he would never go out and buy a mineral egg as a present. Why? "It's not eggs-zactly my thing."

Morey Amsterdam

But actor/comedian Morey Amsterdam had the most unusual collection of the three. It was statuettes of cello players.

"I was raised to be a concert cellist," he said. "My father was a concertmaster of the San Francisco Symphony Orchestra for 35 years. He played the violin and my brother played the piano. With me playing the cello, we had a nice family trio.

"But," he continued, "cello players are hard to find. In real life, I'd say there are about 25 violin players for every cello player, and, in the world of statuettes, it's even worse." Even so, Morey had managed to accumulate an impressive display of them after several years of collecting.

"The difference between a cello player and a bass viol player is that a bass player stands to play his instrument and a cello player sits," he explained.

Actually, Morey began his career at the age of 10 as a boy soprano on a San Francisco radio program. Later, he joined his older brother's vaudeville act as a comedian. He was a comedy writer for Will Rogers, Jack Benny, Fanny Brice, Milton Berle, Rose Marie and Henny Youngman as well as for several United States presidents and heads of state of other countries. He appeared in several movies, television shows, and live theater productions, toured the country with his own comedy act, and gave many concert cello performances, including at the White House.

Chapter 19

My Times with Loni

I could have told Loni Anderson that Burt Reynolds would end up breaking her heart. In fact, I did.

No that I personally disliked Burt Reynolds. Although I had never met him, I thought he was quite a hunk and, no doubt, a "good old boy" in some instances. It's just that I believed women need to recognize the fact that some men seem to lack "staying power" for long-term relationships.

Although it was well known that Loni and Burt had been spending a lot of time together for about three years, she still maintained her own light and airy, two-story fairytale-like house in 1986. Located in the San Fernando Valley, it had pegged wooden floors, a large open kitchen, and a fantasy room to display her own particular keepsakes. But now she had implied that she was planning to sell the house and move in with Burt for good.

Ralph and I were there for a couple of hours to put together an "at-home-with-the-stars" type of article for *Woman's World* magazine. We'd known the down-to-earth, soft-spoken actress for quite some time and we thought she was making a mistake to burn her bridges so drastically.

"Loni, you're just too nice and too trusting for your own good" was how we both outspokenly put it.

Not that she had asked our opinion or even had any reason to care what we thought. In spite of the many warnings she had no doubt received from people who cared about her, and that, according to various publications, Burt had loved and left several attractive, well known movie and television ladies, she seemed to feel that this time he would be different.

Nevertheless, she smiled and shrugged agreeably. In the times I had worked with Loni, I've never known her to be mean or even intolerant.

When, later in 1995, I did a cooking article with her for a *Woman's World* cover story, she made a supreme effort to round up her favorite healthful recipes, hand-copy them, and fax them to my office. I wrote up my story from our telephone interview, faxed it off to the magazine, and made a much-needed $1,000 without even going out the door.

On the above-mentioned day, Ralph and I were wandering about, looking for picture-taking possibilities and discussing some of Loni's favorite things with her.

Previous visits had been involved with articles about her huge collection of *Snow White* memorabilia.

I may have been one of the first -- if not *the* first – to write about Loni's love of *Snow White*, in particular the version created by Walt Disney's artists for his full-length 1937 animated feature.

It came about because Loni – of Swedish and German descent – was born with curly black hair and hazel eyes in a family of blue- and green-eyed blonds. When she played make believe with her sister and three first cousins, she was never allowed to be the princess.

"I felt so different and out of things," she confessed. "Even my father – the only other black-haired member of my family – had blue eyes. But he would read stories to the five of us, and one day he found a Grimm's fairytale that described a princess who had 'skin as white as snow, lips as red as blood, and hair as black as ebony.' He was delighted and so was I. He said to me. 'See, Loni, there *is* a black-haired princess after all. From now on, I'm going to call you Snow White.'"

Later, during the 1950s, Loni's grandmother took her to see a re-release of Disney's *Snow White and the Seven Dwarfs*. After that, she decided she wanted to become an animator, even though she was also interested in acting and had appeared on stage as an Indian princess at the age of 10. She continued to study, both acting and art through her school years.

"My dream was that someday Walt Disney would come to Minnesota and see me drawing and say 'You, I want you,' she told me laughingly.

That dream was never to be. Married, divorced, and with a young daughter to support at the tender age of eighteen, Loni "turned practical," went to college to earn her teacher's degree in art, and actually taught that subject for a while.

After getting her Equity card, Loni found that, due to her naturally dark hair, she was being assigned ethnic roles. And when those parts became scarce as the ethnics, themselves, began filling them, she decided to go blond; but not without regrets.

"I'd been Snow White nearly all of my life and that change really bothered me." she said.

She showed me two cels (original animation drawings on transparent celluloid) which she treasured. One was Disney's black-haired Snow White; the other an animation rendition of herself as the blond comic book character, Daisy Mae (Lil Abner's girlfriend) drawn for her by Bill Mendez.

"I always tell people, this is who I was and this is who I became. But inside, I am still Snow White."

Along with the vast number of figurines, clocks, picture books, dolls, posters, and cards in her Snow White collection, there were several special items. One was an audio tape made especially for her by Adriana Caselotti, the "voice" of Disney's Snow White, at the request of Shirley Jones and Marty Ingalls. Another was a large, hand-decorated porcelain bisque table ornament featuring the black-haired princess serving dinner to her seven little friends.

As Ralph and I wound up the day's work, it became clear that Loni had other things on her mind. Always considerate of guests, she made an effort to contain herself and graciously bid us goodbye. But we were aware that as soon as we drove away, she'd be out the door and off to the man she believed to be her own Prince Charming.

Chapter 20
S is for Sally Struthers and Shelley Duvall

Sally Struthers

Ralph and I especially enjoyed the day we spent at the house of Sally Struthers, best known for her role of Gloria, the daughter of Archie Bunker, portrayed by Carroll O'Conner, in the TV series *All in the Family*. It was to result in a cover story for *Collectibles Illustrated*, featuring the perky blond actress and her look-alike four-year-old daughter, Samantha, on the cover of an issue bursting with a number of our other celebrity collector stories.

Sally lived in an attractive, quite secluded, house in Brentwood, which was said to be a former residence of actress Rita Hayworth. On arrival, the first things we noted were cats that appeared to be standing or scampering across the roof of both her garage and her guest house. On a closer look, we realized that they were merely decorative images. One pair appeared to be black ceramic ones and the others were white.

Oddly, although Sally's very extensive collection of cat items included doorstops, bookends, bowls, planters, cookie jars, lamps, glass, ceramic and cloth cats and a pair of ancient canvas carnival cats created to be knocked over with thrown baseballs, the roof cats had already been there when she moved into her home. Other collections included thimbles from all over the world, antique perfume bottles, and Teddy bears. And she also sought out interesting antiques to add to the eclectic décor of her home. One was a V-shaped hotel or theater lobby seat which she stripped to its natural wood and had reupholstered. Another was a nearly life-size wooden cutout bellboy.

Sally's life to date had been quite unusual. She began her professional career in 1967 as a dancer with Herb Alpert's Tijuana Brass band. Because she'd had no formal dance training, she faked her dance steps at an open audition. At a height of only 5'1", she'd been selected to be a model by well-known modeling agent Nina Blanchard. And she was chosen for the part of Gloria due to a case of laryngitis. At her audition, her hoarse, raspy voice coming out of her tiny frame appealed to Norman Lear's sense of humor and prompted him to choose her over some 200 other candidates.

Sally was known for her many charitable works. She was involved with the International Christian Children's Fund and traveled extensively for that cause to such countries as Africa and Thailand. Her love of children extended to work with those classified as "mentally challenged" as well.

Shelley Duvall

The reason for our interview with Shelley Duvall was her collection of more than a thousand illustrated fairy tale books. And the main reason that collection had become well known to the world was that she was the originator and producer of a Showtime cable television series entitled *Faerie Tale Theatre*, which featured well known actors and actresses portraying fairytale characters. (In fact, the series is available for sale on DVDs today.)

But I must admit that I found the actress herself -- also well known for her role of Olive Oyl in the movie version of *Popeye* and another in one of my favorite scary movies, *The Shining* -- to have a fascination all her own. Described by the media as one who took "quirky and waif-like roles," she was both unusual looking and attractive.

We met in her private office in the Producer's Building at ABC-TV Center in Hollywood, where some of her books were to be found.

Shelley explained that she had begun collecting antique illustrated books at the age of seventeen because she was interested in the illustrators.

"Some of the most beautiful illustrations were for children's books, for fairy tales," she said. "I found that just about all of the illustrators had done a fairytale book and many famous authors have written fairy tales in addition to their adult fiction. A couple of those were Oscar Wilde and Mark Twain. "

Besides enjoying the pictures of her books, Shelley admitted to reading the stories. "Fairy tales are about real life," she told me. "They deal with our hopes and dreams, and things that adults never grow out of. In the old days, they were used to teach children morals and to teach lessons to everyone – not just children. I always find it pleasurable to read them. They have all the plots that Shakespeare had and more."

The actress had taken several of her books along with which to while away her six-month filming sojourn on the island of

Malta during the making of *Popeye*. In her mind's eye, she began picturing her co-star Robin Williams as a delightful Frog Prince. Later, she persuaded him to play that part in one of her fairytale productions.

Shelley allowed herself the privilege of starring in her film versions of *Rapunzel* and *Rumpelstiltskin*. Among the other actors and actresses appearing in her fairy tale series were Liza Minnelli, Christopher Reeves, Mick Jagger, Bernadette Peters, Carrie Fisher, Melissa Gilbert, Tatum O'Neal, Alan Arkin, Teri Garr, Pam Dawber, and John Lithgow.

She said that, even though she had located a number of unusual and little known fairy tales, her own favorites continued to be the traditional ones such as *Snow White, Beauty and the Beast, Sleeping Beauty,* and *Jack and the Beanstalk.*

After writing the article on Shelley Duvall for *Collectibles Illustrated,* I had occasion to write a different, more in-depth version for *The Franklin Mint Almanac.* I was to learn, over the years, that I would often find more than one market for my story ideas and interviews, but I always did a completely different re-write of the material in order to slant it to each one in an appropriate and exclusive manner.

Tippi Hedren with her elephants

Shirley with Glenn Ford

Gale Storm with Shirley

Ray Bolger (the scarecrow) with Shirley

Mel Blanc with Shirley

Morgan Brittany with Scarlet O'Hara doll

Shirley with Jill Whelan

Kim Fields and Baby Sister Alexis

Ken Kercheval and Shirley

Shirley, Adam West (Batman), and Donna Jordan

Sally Struthers and Shirley

Shirley with Michael Gross

Shirley and Michele Lee

Shirley with Shelley Duvall

Pappy Boyington with Shirley

Shirley with Richard Simmons

Shirley with Jonathan Winters

Ray Bradbury with Shirley

Chapter 21

Shari Lewis – A Kid's and a Puppet's Best Friend

What most people don't understand about Shari Lewis is the extent of her talents. She was an actress, dancer, ventriloquist, puppeteer, book author, and a musician and symphony conductor, who performed with and conducted a number of symphony orchestras.

I first saw Shari on television around the time I discovered Captain Kangaroo, following the birth of my oldest son, David in 1961. Getting up with a baby in the wee hours of the morning causes you to seek company, and early morning television came into our lives for that reason. Not that the baby watched; *we* did!

It was Bob's turn to get up with our little darling. When I joined him in the living room, where he was sleepily-eyeing the set, he told me that he'd turned on the TV and there was this big, strange-looking guy tippy-toeing around lighting candles on a birthday cake. The Captain became a regular "friend" after that, and, subsequently, so did Shari. She had introduced Lamb Chop to the public on that show in 1957 and later gone on to do a children's show of her own. I was fascinated by her pert little face, her bright personality, her clever dance numbers, and her energy.

I first *met* Shari in 1983 on an assignment for *Collectibles Illustrated*. It was thought that her vast number of puppets would make a cute collector story.

As Ralph and I entered her gracious two story Beverly Hills home, which she shared with her husband, book publisher Jeremy Tarcher, we noticed what looked like collector's item type puppets on the living room walls.

Shari entered, wearing pants and an appropriate white cotton print blouse featuring stylized marionettes on strings. "The material was given to me by my hairdresser and I had the blouse made," she explained.

She said that her puppet collection was mainly a working one. "I don't generally like to hang onto things for which I have no use, so I often give away the ones I don't really care about."

This caused us a moment of concern until we entered the room where she had laid out a selection for Ralph to photograph. Although she assured us that this was only about half of her puppets, they covered her ping-pong table completely and there were more, life-size ones standing behind it.

Sherry said that her very first puppet had been a turn-of-the-century hard dummy called "Willie Talk." It had been given to her by a performer friend of her father when she began to study ventriloquism as a teenager. Shari's dad was a college professor, who had been dubbed "New York City's official magician" by Mayor La Guardia. When he learned that his young daughter could "throw her voice," he arranged for her to take lessons with a former vaudevillian. She began with wooden dummies, but discovered that cuddly hand-puppets were more her style. After that, she gave Willie away.

"Á puppet," she told us, "is not just a static piece of equipment. It's a creature who either comes to life for you or it doesn't. If it doesn't, there's really no reason to keep it."

She related the story behind her relationship with her best-known hand-puppet.

"When I got this lamb puppet, I sat in front of a mirror with it and imagined that it wanted something from me and that I had a firm reason why the lamb couldn't have it. Then she immediately came to life for me. I still feel closest of all to Lamb Chop."

Ralph and I had never seen Shari's nightclub act so we were surprised when she showed us her life-size "Fred Astaire" and two "chorus ladies."

"In my act, I explain that instead of being a puppeteer, I had planned to be a dancer who would one day appear on the screen with Fred Astaire," she said. "Then I run offstage and return to dance with this puppet."

She showed us how she also danced with her chorus ladies, fashioned with a piece of equipment that swung across her shoulders like a milkmaid's yoke so that, on either side of her, they seemed to kick in unison with her.

Shari was most favorably impressed with the work of Jim Hensen of Muppet fame. And her choice for the best puppet she'd ever seen was the Yoda puppet of the *Star Wars* movies.

Following this visit, about ten years were to go by before I found a reason to talk with Shari again. By then she'd been enriching the lives of children and their parents for more than 30 years with varied TV shows, 61 children's books, and about 20 videos. She'd performed at the annual White House Christmas party for the children of the Diplomatic Corps and emceed the annual

White House Easter Festival for four years. She'd served on the national board of the Girl Scouts and the international board of the Boy Scouts, received a Peabody Award and the John F. Kennedy Center Award for Excellence and Creativity. And most recently, she had been testifying before Congress for the FCC about enforcing the Children's Television Act.

My assignment was to talk with her about children and families for a publication called *Family Times*. Closing our discussion, I had one question left for this mother of grownup daughter, writer/producer Mallary Tarcher. It was what she considered the best way to relate to young children.

Her answer was short and to the point. "Just look them in the eye and talk to them 'regular.'"

Chapter 22

Some Star Trek Guys

DeForest Kelley

It was still in the 1970s when I interviewed actor DeForest Kelley, also known as Doctor Leonard "Bones" McCoy, for a children's magazine. The original *Star Trek* TV series was in re-runs, a full-length *Star Trek* movie was in the making, and a new *Star Trek II* television series was soon to air.

As one of the original cast members to voyage on the Starship Enterprise, DeForest Kelley was easily recognized wherever he went. If my sons had been home when he arrived at our house for my interview, I'm sure they would have been delighted to meet him. Our dog was another matter.

Not that our chunky little off-white half Malemute, half Norwegian Elkhound pup, Misty, was uncertain. She seemed pleasantly excited when the handsome six-footer (made taller yet by his choice of cowboy boots) entered our living room and remarked on how cute she was. Then again, he might have frightened her a little. At any rate, she proceeded to pee on the hearth of the fireplace, causing me immediate embarrassment.

Too bad I hadn't gone to *his* house, I thought. Maybe *he* would have had something to be embarrassed about.

I understood the cowboy boots when he confessed that, as a child, he had preferred playing cowboys and Indians to pretending to be a spaceman. Born in a small town in Georgia, Dee (as he said he liked to be called) was the son of a Baptist minister. After becoming an actor, he played villains, psychopaths and western "heavies," so did have a chance to be a cowboy, at least on film. And he often went horseback riding for pleasure.

He said that, up until the day he joined the *Star Trek* cast, he had never even been interested in science fiction. However, the more involved he became, the more exciting it was for him.

One of his favorite memories was related to "Tribbles," the artificial, but supposedly alive, little furry creatures of many colors featured in one *Star Trek* episode.

"They had been left here and there all over the set and it had gotten to be kind of a gag," he told me. "You'd find one in your boot or some other unlikely place. Finally, I decided to have some fun of my own with them. The script called for me to "perform surgery" on Spock's father and it was a very tense moment. I reached down into what was supposed to be his stomach and pulled out a Tribble and I said, "The trouble with him is that he's got a Tribble inside him."

The entire cast broke up over that. However, it became just another 'out-take' and, of course, was never seen on the actual television show.

Walter Koenig

Walter Koenig, who portrayed Engineer Pavel Chekov in the *Star Trek* TV series and movies, was emphatic in telling Ralph and me that he collected books and other items featuring *comic strip characters*, but did *not* collect comic *books*.

Entering the den in his San Fernando Valley home, we could see what he meant. Floor-to-ceiling, wall-to-wall shelves held his 600 volume Big Little Book collection and similar books, all based on comic strip characters. There were also colorful comic character statuettes of plastic, wood, or lead, a 700 item collection of comic character pinback buttons, and individual items having to do with that category, including a Mickey Mouse telephone.

Walter began collecting the Big Little Books as a young boy living in Manhattan.

"They first came out in the 1930s and '40s," he explained. "I started buying them in the '40s in the five-and-ten-cent stores. By the time they stopped making them, I had about 150. When I went off to college, my mom got rid of them, but in 1967, my wife gave me one she found at a Hollywood bookstore for a present. And that started me off all over again."

Since I was of the same generation as Walter, I remembered them well. About three-by-four inches in size, by an inch to an inch-and-a-half thick, they generally had about 400 pages, with one picture page to every one of text.

Walter told us that early ones were about Mickey Mouse and Dick Tracy. He had books about Lil Abner, Flash Gordon, Donald Duck, Popeye, Superman, Gang Busters, Jungle Jim, and many more. He said he believed they stopped making them for a while around 1948, but that more were published at a later date. And another publisher created the Little Big Books, of which he had some as well.

An especially prized item was a foot-and-a-half figure of himself as Chekov standing in a miniature transporter waiting to be beamed up.

Walter had a number of other collections, and his son Joshua (fourteen-years-old at that time) collected *Star Wars* items. His actress wife, Judy Levitt, and their then ten-year-old daughter, Danielle, both chose to be supportive "non-collectors."

Known as an actor, writer, teacher, and director, Walter Koenig had already written a book of his own entitled *Chekov's Enterprise*.

Chapter 23

Fields and Franklin

Kim Fields

Over the years, I've interviewed kids from eight to eighteen, and even younger on some occasions. The trick is to take the things they tell you as seriously as you would any adult and never talk down to them.

The reason Ralph and I visited the Los Angeles area home of then teenage Kim Fields was because of her collection of hats. The fifteen-year-old actress, best known at that time for her role of Tootie on the television series, *The Facts of Life*, had dozens of them of all styles and colors.

Kim's mom, actress/producer Chip Fields, was also there. In those days, she was appearing periodically as Tootie's mother on the above-mentioned show.

Kim told us that her "prize" was a "Michael Jackson hat," which she had recently acquired when she recorded *Dear Michael*, a song dedicated to that world-renowned superstar. Although she had known the Jackson family for some time, this particular hat story was something which caused her to glow in the telling.

"It's at least ten years old and was worn by Michael for the album cover of his first hit solo record *Got To Be There*. He used three of those hats in all and today he has one, Mo Town kept one, and they gave this one to me," she said, plopping it on her head and posing prettily. "It's my best collector's item."

Her collection included a painter's cap, a safari helmet, and a fedora given to her by her co-star, Nancy McKeon. There was an official Yankees hat sent to her by the team, and a Pittsburgh Pirates hat given to her by her father.

Another favorite was a white cap she'd purchased in San Diego that had a story of its own. A devoted fan of singer Patti La-Belle, she'd attended the San Diego Jazz Festival with friends to see her perform.

"A security guard took us across the baseball stadium and up to the stage to see Patti," Kim related. "She'd acknowledged me before when I watched her perform at the Beverly Theatre. She spotted me and called out, 'Hey, Kim,' and told me to come backstage to see her. Since I wanted her autograph and didn't have anything else for her to sign, I took off my hat and asked her to sign it." She grinned. "I plan to have people autograph my hats whenever possible. "

During our visit, we had the fun of meeting Kim's two-year-old sister, Alexis, who joined in trying on hats and posing for Ralph's camera.

As often happened, we had another occasion to visit the Fields family. It was nine years later and we were there to interview 11-year-old Alexis, who had been chosen to portray the role of Sheila on one of her favorite TV shows named *Roc*.

She told us that her favorite sport was swimming. She also said that big sister Kim never gave her any advice about acting. "But she does give me advice about how to live my life," she remarked. "She says I should never change and never get a big head."

Bonnie Franklin

Ralph and I had fun with Bonnie Franklin, best known at that time for her role of Ann Romano on the *One Day at a Time* TV series.

The first time we interviewed her was for *Collectibles Illustrated*. We met in her dressing room at Universal Studios where she was working at the time. But we were to write about her more than once and other times we went to her house.

Bonnie's collection was one of red-haired dolls.

"But I don't just want dolls that have red hair," she explained. "I want strange dolls that have red hair…unusual dolls. To use a Norman Lear expression, I want dolls that have 'wet faces,' meaning faces in which you can see everything happening."

Although Bonnie had never played with dolls as a child, people began giving her red-haired dolls during the making of her before-mentioned series and, as she put it, "Before I knew it, I was collecting."

Of course the idea had been to give red-haired dolls to a redhead, but Bonnie was quick to admit that she was not a natural one.

"My grandfather was a redhead, but my hair color comes out of a bottle," she confessed. "I first changed the color for a particular stage role."

On the day at the studio, she told us, "My dolls are just like little people to me. Just today a funny thing happened. When I went to put these dolls in a bag to bring them here to the studio, I found myself unconsciously being very careful to place them with their heads out of the bag. I was worried that they would not be able to breathe."

Bonnie also favored unusual antique items among her home furnishings. For example, there was a dark wooden church pew in her front hallway and a very old French antique child's rocking horse in her office. She used a French cradle as a living room planter and an old sea chest for holding firewood.

Many of her red-haired dolls "lived" on her living room mantle and a red-haired witch doll dangled among the copper-bottomed pots and pans in the kitchen. Other dolls included a red-haired Carmen Miranda doll, a Peter Pan doll, an ugly-faced can-can dancer, a long-legged ballerina, and a Little Lulu doll..

"I feel good looking at my dolls," she told us. "There's something terribly non-stuffy...very unglamorous and down-to-earth about them. They help to keep me humble!"

Chapter 24

We Meet with Super Heroes

Adam West

Since *Collectibles Illustrated* featured stories about collectors and collectibles of every description, Ralph and I were often asked to do stories on people who were not collectors, but well known for their roles in certain categories of entertainment that resulted in collectibles.

One issue dealt with collectibles having to do with Batman.

That was how we first met Adam West, who portrayed that role in the humorous, tongue-in-cheek , highly-rated *Batman* TV series which ran from 1966-1968, as well as the 1966 *Batman* movie.

We interviewed Adam, alias Batman, alias Bruce Wayne, also-known-as Bill (his real name) in the den of his family home at that time in the Los Angeles Pacific Palisades area. The immediate family included his wife, Marcelle, and their six children – two of hers, two of his, and two of theirs.

Although he had gone on to a number of other roles by that time, he was still Batman to his many fans and had made personal appearances as that character all over the world.

"I enjoy playing Batman more than any role I've ever done," he said. "But I wouldn't do it quite the same way if I had another

opportunity and could choose. I'd attempt to make him less frivolous and silly, though still keeping the humor. "

Three different actresses had played Catwoman in those versions of *Batman*. They were Julie Newmar, Lee Merriweather and
Eartha Kitt.

Of Newmar, Adam said, "One of my favorite segments with
her was when she falls to her doom and I, as Batman, was left
sadly holding her glove. I still have that glove among my collectibles," he added.

Among the many celebrities who guest-starred as far-out villains
back then were Liberace, Cesar Romero, Vincent Price, Otto Preminger,
George Sanders, Burgess Meredith, Frank Gorshin and John Astin.

Although Adam had "a wonderful stunt double," he chose to
do some of his own stunt work with the Batmobile and the Bat-
boat in order to preserve the line of movement of the character.
Action scenes were made more difficult because he had the costume to contend with. The mask, for example, did not allow for pe-
ripheral vision and did not entirely turn with his head. Since it was
the only one of its kind in existence – made of impact plastic with
a foam lining and fairly light, though hot inside – it was insured for
a million dollars and required that he take good care of it.

Adam's life before *Batman* was reasonably exciting. He grew
up on a wheat ranch near Walla Walla, Washington, worked as a
writer, director and announcer for a network in Sacramento, spent
two years in the U.S. Army, hitchhiked through Europe, did radio
and TV work and piloted tourists in Hawaii. He said that, as a kid,
he read the *Batman* comic books and could still recall his early
impressions of that character.

Ralph and I had entertained *Collectibles Illustrated* editor

Charles J. Jordan and his wife, Donna, with lunch at the Beverly Hills Hotel Polo Lounge during their visit to the Los Angeles area. Sometime later, after this interview with Adam West, Donna returned alone for a visit with friends in the area. For a treat, we decided to see if Adam would agree to meet with her.

As a result, Donna Jordan, Ralph and I met and had lunch with Adam West at a popular seafood restaurant on the beach, where he posed for personal pictures with us.

Kirk Alyn

For the *Superman* issue of the magazine, Ralph and I met with Kirk Alyn, --the first actor to play Superman on screen in the 1948 film serial *Superman* and its sequel, *Atom Man vs. Superman* -- for a lunchtime interview at an outdoor Hollywood restaurant.

Each of those serials had run for five years in movie theaters across this country and overseas. Although that had been thirty years before, the six-foot-two-inch now grey-haired gentleman was still impressive enough to turn the heads of the diners in the patio.

"I did all of my own stunts," he told us. "That included carrying Noel Neill, who played Lois Lane in both the movie and the later television show. Even though she was small, it was exhausting, since I had to do it over and over."

As to flying, at first it was done with wires, a harness, and a breastplate, but the wires proved to be too obvious. Next, they had Kirk stand, looking up at the ceiling with a fan blowing down on him and smoke pots creating moving clouds. The camera was turned on its side, and later reversed so that he appeared to be flying horizontally.

Noel Neill and Jack Larson

Ralph and I met with Noel Neill, who played Lois Lane, and Jack Larson, who played Jimmy Olsen in the 1950s *Superman* television series at Laird International Studios (once RKO Pathé) in Culver City.

Although Kirk Alyn had been invited to play Superman on television, he had declined, and character actor George Reeves had accepted the part.

"The biggest memory I have of playing Jimmy is that I was always tied to a chair with a bomb at my feet, as was Lois, and George would break through walls to rescue us," said Jack. "Inevitably, I would say on cue, 'Golly, Superman, I thought you were never going to get here.'"

Although George did fly on wires at first, there was a time when they broke and dropped him on his bottom. When that happened, he wasn't seriously hurt but his feelings were. So other methods were used after that; one being to have him hit a springboard and jump over the camera onto a mattress. For a landing scene, he'd leap off a high ladder, grab a bar placed beyond the camera and swing in over it.

Noel told us that her favorite show was the one in which she dreamed she was going to marry Superman.

The show ended abruptly due to the death of George Reeves. By that time, Noel was married, so she decided to retire. But at the time of our interview, she was divorced and accepting acting rolls again. Jack had become a partner to writer-producer-director James Bridges of Skyway Productions.

After that issue of the magazine came out, Noel Neill wrote a letter to Charles Jordan, Editor (which I have today) telling him that she was writing for both Jack Larson and herself, and wished to compliment the magazine for its "excellent Superman article. We both feel it is the best that has ever been written on us and George Reeves and the photography is also very good," she said.

Chapter 25
French and Gross

Victor French

These days, with TV series re-runs available every day of the week on Cable television, fans are frequently able to see some of their favorite actors who have already passed on. Such is the case with Victor French who guest starred in thirty-nine TV series, portrayed Mr. Edwards in *Little House on the Prairie,* Chief Mobey in *Carter Country,* appeared on *Gunsmoke* 13 times in various roles, and even made it to *Bonanza* a few times. In addition he played Agent 44 on *Get Smart.*

When Ralph and I visited the dark-haired, bearded actor at his San Fernando Valley home, we learned that he was a very enthusiastic movie buff. The den walls of his home were made colorful by rows of framed theater lobby cards featuring cowboy actors dating back to the early days of motion pictures.

He told us that he began collecting movie star postcards as a small boy and had about 1000 of them at that time. He also had lobby cards of Academy Award winning films and pictures and posters of his favorite non-western actors and actresses.

The son of a Hollywood stuntman, Victor grew up in the

movie business and said he could count a lot of the "old-timers" among his personal friends. "Eddie Dean and Jimmy Wakely both changed my diapers."

"My dad worked for the Flying A Movie Studios. He rode horses off of cliffs and bridges and did fights and saddle falls. He played "heavies" in Westerns.

"I've been target shooting and motorcycle riding with Roy Rogers and have a pair of his old boots that he autographed for me," he said happily. "I also have boots that belonged to Tom Mix and a hat that belonged to Buck Jones. And I spent two hours talking with Randolph Scott."

He enjoyed getting together with friends to spend several hours at a time watching video tapes of old Western movies.

"They were called 'programmers' and were made very fast, but they all had a moral and a theme. My collection is all based on wonderful memories about values in living that the movies taught me."

Victor began his own acting career as a stunt rider just like his dad. And, in 1966, he and his father, Ted, both appeared on a *Gunsmoke* episode. He also directed some of the episodes of *Little House on the Prairie*. He is said to have been a close and valued friend to the late Michael Landon.

Victor French died of lung cancer in 1989, at the age of 54. In 1998, he was inducted into the Western Performers Hall of Fame at the National Cowboy and Western Heritage Museum in Oklahoma City, Oklahoma.

Michael Gross

Michael Gross was one of the people we visited more than once over a period of several years. Besides being well known for his role of Steven Keaton on the TV series *Family Ties*, he's one of the stars in the movie *Tremors* and its several sequels.

The first time we interviewed Michael, his collection consisted largely of keepsake items having to do with his paternal grandfather, Chester Gross, a switch engine foreman and fifty-six-year employee of the Atchison, Topeka & Santa Fe Railroad in Fort Madison, Iowa.

Born in Chicago, Illinois, Michael spent childhood summers visiting his grandparents.

He told us about one special memory of those times.

"I was about four years old and I was standing with my grandfather near the locomotive 'ready track,' where the engines steamed up and waited to go out on the next freight or passenger train. I heard the steam safety valve pop at a decibel-splitting level and I remember being frightened to death and just plastering myself against his leg with both arms wrapped around his thigh. The huge black locomotives were standing there – one wheel of which towered over me – and, indeed, was taller than a six foot man.

"My grandfather would take me onto the switch engine and the crews would take care of me," he recalled. "He'd let me climb all over things, and one time I stayed on for a couple of hours, riding uptown with them."

Michael treasured his grandfather's railroad watch and brass switch keys. He also had a ticket validater, hats, lanterns, spikes, track bolts, thermometers, linens, ticket stubs, maps, brochures,

Santa Fe calendar art from the 1920s and 1930s, timetables, menus and postcards. He even had special Santa Fe dining car china.

"I ate off of it at my grandparents' house," he said. "The employees were allowed to take home any flawed or chipped dishes and my grandfather would eat his morning prunes from a Santa Fe bowl."

Michael's wife, Elza, also loves trains and agreed to hold their wedding reception in a private railroad car bound for San Juan Capistrano, California.

Some years later we visited the couple at the sprawling ranch-style house surrounded by a large, shady flower-filled yard featuring an immense, four-hundred-year-old oak tree, to which they had moved by then.

Here there was room for several larger collectibles, including an antique railroad baggage car, parlor car chairs, and a large roll-top desk that once belonged to a high-up Santa Fe official, a wood-burning caboose stove, a station bench, a pair of order hoops once used for handing written messages to workers on a moving train as it passed through the station, and an ancient courtesy wheelchair for the infirm.

At last count, Michael had become part-owner of the Santa Fe Southern Railway, which operates between Lamy and Santa Fe, New Mexico. He has been a spokesperson for Operation Lifesaver, a campaign promoting safety at railroad grade crossings. And, as of 2009, he became a celebrity spokesperson for the B & O Railroad Museum in Baltimore, Maryland.

Chapter 26

Bugs Bunny's Best Friend

Without Mel Blanc, would Bugs Bunny have become as popular as he has been over the years? Not only did Mel do his talking for him, but he designed the *way* that he spoke. Mel explained to those who would listen that he was not an impersonator, but a voice *creator*.

The first time I met with Mel was on assignment for *the Franklin Mint Almanac* , before I had really connected with Ralph. They supplied the photographer, so I drove alone to the home of Mel's son, Noel, where our major purpose was to meet with father and son to discuss their collection of rare and valuable watches.

Later, I visited Mel at his own Pacific Palisades home with Ralph, to produce further articles on the subject. But, of course, the topic of Bugs Bunny and some of the other voices for which he was best known, always came up.

"It was back in the 1930s when I originated the voice for Bugs Bunny," Mel said. "Since they told me that he was 'a tough little stinker,' I devised a combination of what I thought of as the two toughest voices around – Brooklyn and the Bronx. For Pepé le Pew, the amorous skunk, I came up with a French accent similar to actor

Charles Boyer. Little Tweety Bird needed an innocent baby voice, and the big, sloppy cat Sylvester had to have a big, sloppy voice."

Some of the other 400 different characters for whom he fashioned and delivered dialogue were Yosemite Sam, Foghorn Leghorn, Porky Pig, Daffy Duck, Wile E. Coyote, and Barney Rubble of *The Flintstones.*

Mel told me that when Noel was a little boy, he would read the Sunday newspaper comics to him, using different voices for each of the characters. Eventually, he taught the voices of the many characters he represented to Noel, who has followed in his father's footsteps and eventually replaced him in the business.

Time and timing had always been important to Mel, who was not only adept at ad-libbing his own remarks, but knew instinctively how much time to allow for them. It was a knack he was believed to have developed during radio's golden age in the 1930s and 1940s ,when he starred in his own show, and appeared as guest of comedians like Jack Benny, Abbot and Costello, and Burns and Allen.

"Dad's got a built-in clock in his head," Noel told us fondly. "Producers would tell him to do something in 30 seconds and he'd do it in 29 and know that he had."

Ralph and I were privileged to meet Mel's wife, Estelle, who insisted upon making lunch for us to eat with Mel on the closed-in back porch. She put together a yummy tuna salad, which I gobbled happily, but Ralph politely declined.

We learned that she was the one who began the watch collection in 1946, after having been a witness to Mel's preoccupation with watches in jewelry store windows. For his birthday, she selected a gold-encased Patek Philippe watch from a Venice, California antique shop.

Mel had heard of Patek Philippe – a Swiss company founded in the 1800s and greatly respected for magnificent complicated watches. Still, he was appalled to discover that Estelle had paid $375 for a "used" watch, no matter how handsome and how distinguished its origin. He was somewhat mollified, however, upon discovering how ingenious his new timepiece was.

"I didn't even have to look at the watch to tell time," he explained. "When I pressed the little lever, it rang the hour, double-chimed for quarter hours and single-chimed for the minutes. It was a rare minute repeater." Later, he learned that such a watch in a New York Tiffany's store was priced at more than $2,000.

Mel told us that in the early days of portable clocks, they were called 'carrying timepieces.'

"They earned their new name by association with town watchmen, who took small clocks on straps with them on their rounds of duty. Since the rounds were called 'watches,' the small clocks also came to be known by that term."

Their widely varied and historically interesting watch collection was generally stored in bank vaults, and the Blancs kept track of them through a comprehensive file of enlarged, detailed photos. But, during my visits, I was able to examine many of them and hear stories and details that made it so special. And our conversation with the Blancs was seasoned with many great names from the who's who of watch making.

In the midst of all those treasures, Ralph and I could also spot some of the more personal ones. Mel's many awards and documents included the carbon microphone award of the Pacific Pioneer Broadcasters, a Congressional citation offering "special recognition to Mel Blanc, whose voice has brought joy to the world," and an Oscar willed to Mel by a producer, since Oscars were not presented to voice people. A Bugs Bunny statue was given to him instead.

The early Warner Bros. cartoons concluded with the words "That's all Folks." A few years after our last interview, Mel Blanc surprised me by mailing me an advanced proof copy of his auto-biographical book, entitled *That's not all Folks!* with an endearing personal autograph.

Chapter 27
From Antiquities to Elephants

Here are some more of the celebrities who had collections of things interesting enough for *Collectibles Illustrated* stories.

John Saxon

This handsome star of many movies for theaters and television, as well as several TV series, began accumulating Etruscan antiquities while visiting Italy following the filming of his first movie, *The Reluctant Debutante* co-starring Rex Harrison, Kay Kendall and Sandra Dee, on location in Paris.

Born Carmine Orrico in Brooklyn, New York, John told us that his parents had both migrated from different parts of Italy.

"My father was raised in Salerno in an area where the Etruscans had lived, so I have good reason to believe that I might be descended from them."

And though his light and airy California canyon home sported colorful impressionistic paintings representing his interest in modern art, they proved to be a background for pottery pieces whose origins preceded the coming of Christ.

John showed us a wide variety of items from his collection.

Picking up a gracefully curving pink bowl-like object with four rounded corners, he said, "This little lamp is from Biblical times – about the time of Abraham. Oil was placed in the center and wicks came out of the sides. It must have burned with a lot of smoke."

A three foot high human figure puppet suspended from the ceiling by his fireplace was acquired while John was making an Italian movie in Salerno in 1972.

"I went to see a puppet theater that was said to be the oldest existing one in the world, operated as a family tradition," he remarked. "The show was about Saracens invading Sicily, with knights and sword fights and all that. I talked them into letting me buy a couple of puppets they no longer used, which are at least 100 years old and were made by their family members."

He demonstrated the workings of the puppet we had seen. "The arms move and the head opens up and imitation blood pours out when it's struck by another puppet's sword."

Ken Kercheval

Ken Kercheval, who is still probably best known for his portrayal of Cliff Barnes in the *Dallas* TV series, showed us a wide variety of his collectibles, including American art, glassware, Packard cars, Civil War and antique political items, Abraham Lincoln memorabilia, rural America Paintings, vintage parade torches.aad other 'curiosities.'

He said, "I once flew all night from Los Angeles to Cincinnati , drove to an auction in Indiana, and, by 11:30 a.m.. had doled out a large number of dollars for every collectible item there that I wanted. I was walking out the door when a dealer I knew was just arriving. I told him, 'Robert, forget it. I've got it.'"

One interesting item was an old hand-wrought pitchfork that had been stuck in the ground, had a tree grow up around it, and had a piece of the tree stump still clinging to it.

Another was Lincoln's personal chamber pot for which Ken had phoned in his bid and been thrilled to be told that he had won. We were a bit dubious about his choice of that honor, but couldn't help but admire its pretty purple color and presidential seal.

Ralph and I returned to Ken's house more than once to produce additional articles about his collections. For publications about automobiles, we concentrated on the vintage Packards he'd discovered in such places as Augusta, Omaha, Santa Barbara, Santa Fe, and Terre Haute and given the names of those locations.

John Larroquette

It was fun meeting John Larroquette after seeing him on one of the shows that Bob and I liked to watch – *Night Court*, in which he played a lawyer named Dan Fielding.

Ralph and I pulled up before what TV Guide referred to as "a sprawling ranch house on a hilltop overlooking the Pacific Ocean." I couldn't have described it better.

We were there to discuss John's hobby of collecting rare first editions of modern books. The first thing we learned was that the books were so rare that few people had even heard about his all-time favorite author – a poet named Charles Bukowski.

John said, "He lived in the underbelly of society, yet had the power and discipline to show it to us, unlike most derelicts who gwt swept away by the street cleaners. He was a racetrack freak and his words are filthy by society's norms, but they reach out to me."

The 6'4" actor told us that he loved looking at a work in the pristine star in which it was first published, and many of his books – which were very valuable – were published in extremely limited conditions, with exceptionally fine bindings and illustrations.

Some of his favorite authors included Dylan Thomas, Peter O'Toole, Ernest Hemingway, Hart Crane, Eugene O'Neil and Truman Capote.

Born in New Orleans, John — "a great Beattles fan" — Studied Clarinet and saxophone, loved to write, and considered becoming a priest. He won a scholarship in drama, but joined the Naval Reserve and did a year of active duty in Pensacola, Florida.

Later, he worked as a bartender and disc jockey, enrolled in a Los Angeles acting school, and began appearing in some local productions and doing some TV work. His first co-starring TV series role was in NBC's *Baa Baa Black Sheep*. In 1983, He got his *Night Court* role.

John and his wife, Elizabeth, had two children at the time of our interview, but a third was born at a later date.

John's credits are far too numerous to mention here and, of course, he was seen several times on *The Tonight Show*, *David Letterman*, and *Saturday Night Live*.

As a mystery enthusiast, I was thrilled when I discovered John starring in his courtroom-based series entitled *McBride*, which may also be seen in reruns.

Norm Crosby

Comedian Norm Crosby's collection was both smaller and simpler, but he loved it just the same.

First, let me tell you some of the things I learned about Norm himself.

It seemed that for some years, he had been considered "Mr. Dependable" in the realm of comedians, since he was famous for always coming through with plenty of laughs. He performed in popular nightclubs, concert halls, and theaters-in-the-round, as well as top TV variety shows.

But before that he had been an art student and then in the United States Coast Guard, where he was assigned as a radar operator in the North Atlantic on anti-submarine patrol. At that time he developed a hearing problem caused by concussion from depth charges. After that, he worked in a shoe store and eventually became its manager.

Having quit that job to become a professional comedian, he found that he needed a specialty to be successful. One day, when he happened to listen to an acquaintance who unintentionally "fractured" the English language with malaprops, Norm was so enchanted by what he heard that he decided to develop his comedy routines around the misuse of words through confusion caused by the resemblance in sound. Thus he became known as "The Master of Malaprops."

He confessed that his collection, which had brought us to his home on assignment, actually belonged to his wife, Joan Foley Crosby. It seemed that collecting elephants had run in her family, beginning with her grandparents, then her mother, and now

Joan, who claimed a house just wasn't a home without an elephant collection.

Norm, who made frequent contributions to the collection, said he had an elephant story of his own.

He told us that when he was just starting out as a comedian, the cashier in the coffee shop of a hotel where he was staying in Washington D.C. gave him a little gold elephant.

"She told me that several years before, when she was a hotel clerk in one of the big Washington hotels where Bob Hope sometimes stayed, the actor himself had given it to her. She said that since he claimed his good luck charm to be an elephant, he was wishing her good luck, too, by giving one to her. She said, 'I want to give it to you so that it will bring you the same good luck that Bob Hope had.'

"I took it and put it in my tuxedo pocket. That was in the 1950s and, believe it or not, I have never done a show since then without that little elephant in my pocket. I've even held up a show so that I could go back to my room and get it."

Joan said that her family belief was also that the elephant was a good luck charm, though she was more explicit.

"The elephant must have its trunk up and it should be facing into the house to bring the good luck in."

Norm explained that he always tried to bring Joan an elephant home from whatever faraway place he visited, including India, Uruguay and Israel.

"Shopping for an elephant gives me something to do in my spare time when I need to travel," he said, "but the difficult part is making sure that the one I choose has its trunk up."

Chapter 28
We Meet with Literary "Stars"

While still working for *Collectibles Illustrated*, Ralph and I had occasion to do stories on three of the world's most famous authors for the reason that they were all collectors of something.

Ray Bradbury

We found Ray Bradbury to be very friendly and jolly.

The first thing he told us when we arrived at his Los Angeles area office was, "I collect anything that has to do with fantasy and science fiction, and each thing was collected for a certain reason. They include toys, paintings, posters, and a variety of other items."

He said he read his first science fiction book at the age of six and began collecting *Buck Rogers* comic strips when he was in the fourth grade. Because his classmates made fun of him, he tore them up. Then, a month later, burst into tears because of what he had done.

"From then on, I decided not to let others interfere with my choices. So I began collecting again and made my life whole," he exclaimed.

He told us that he seldom threw anything out and didn't categorize them.

"I'm not neat," he admitted. "I keep things everywhere."

By the time of our interview, Ray had more than 400 published short stories, about twenty novels and numerous screenplays and theater plays to his credit. His works included *The Martian Chronicles*, *Fahrenheit 451* and the 1998 film, *The Wonderful Ice Cream Suit*. He also planned the basic scenario for the United States Pavilion at the New York World's Fair in 1964 and served as consultant on EPCOT at Disney World in Florida, providing a dramatic "outline-blueprint-scenario" for the Spaceship Earth Building.

He still had his *Buck Rogers* comic strips along with early panels of the *Tarzan* ones, a poster of *King Kong*, a painting of a dinosaur toppling a lighthouse used to illustrate his story, *The Fog*, in *The Saturday Evening Post*, and a *Buck Rogers* toy disintegrator gun he acquired though a cereal box-top sendoff.

Ray and his wife had four daughters.

A few years after my first visit with Ray Bradbury, I arranged for him to be a speaker for a chapter of The California Writers' Club, to which I belonged at the time.. The catch was that my husband, Bob, and I had to drive into Los Angeles and pick him up; then return him home after the meeting, since he had never acquired a driver's license.

Louis L'Amour

Having written to request an interview with Louis L'Amour regarding what I had been told was his extensive collection of kachimas, I received a letter from him, denying any such large collection,

but agreeing to an interview, with the warning that "I am somewhat crotchety, have thinning white hair that sometimes stands
on end, and a thinning beard."

He also wrote "At one time I used to collect girls and loved it,
but being a married man who takes it seriously, my activities in
that direction have been curtailed. Now I gather books on subjects that interest me…"

And gather books he did. At that time, he had some 9,000 of
them., but I later learned he had increased it to 10,000.

When Ralph and I went to his Beverly Hills home, we saw evidence of his past bout as a professional boxer in that he had a
large punching bag in the gym he'd made from his former garage.

Born Louis Dearborn LaMoore into a pioneer family in James-
town, North Dakota, he later changed the spelling of his name. He
left school and home at the age of 15 to begin such adventures
as working on ranches , in mines and in lumber camps, meeting
outlaws, journeying to the Orient as an able seaman, and, at the
start of World War II, serving in the United States Army.,

We sat in his thirty-foot-long study and looked at the twelve-
foot-high walls of bookshelves, which he had designed to slide open
and reveal that they were actually double walls of bookshelves.

By then there were more than eighty of his own books in print.
Although termed a writer of "Westerns," he considered them "historical novels," and was also branching out into other areas such
as the American Revolutionary and Civil Wars.

He told us about going to the White House to accept the
Medal of Freedom presented to him by President Ronald Reagan.

"I came up behind him on the side he wasn't expecting and
he turned around and said, 'You're just like Bowdrie,'"

Louis smiled in appreciation. "That's one of my characters and it showed he had read some of my books."

Irving Wallace

At the time when Ralph and I visited Irving Wallace in the huge beamed and book-lined study of his Brentwood home, he was considered one of the five most widely read authors in the world.

Nevertheless, he delighted in collecting personal possessions, autographs, and first editions of other well-known writers with whom he felt a particular kinship.

Some of the most interesting included a rosewood and pearl traveling desk used from 1832 to 1870 by Charles Dickens. He told us that as soon as he had acquired it, he sat right down and tried it out.

"That was the whole point," he said. "When I go to museums to look at things, I can't touch them. When I buy them for myself, I purchase that privilege."

Another favorite find was a fold-up desk and a pipe that had belonged to Arthur Conan Doyle, originator of *Sherlock Holmes*.

Besides a large selection of "popular" books such as *Gone With the Wind*, *Tarzan of the Apes*, *Dracula*, and *Dr. Jekyll and Mr. Hyde*, all signed by their authors, he said that he often bought something that was connected with a book that he himself had written. Those included a small plastic bottle of holy water from Lourdes, the setting of his novel, *The Miracle*, and a tiny (pageless) blown glass reproduction of his book *The Man*.

In addition, he had a varied collection of artworks of famous artists that included Toulouse-Lautrec, Picasso, Chagall, and Diego Rivera.

My first article about this famous author was for *Collectibles Illustrated*. Some years later, he graciously allowed me to write an as-told-to article in which he talked about other authors' books that he considered "page-turners" for *Aim Plus*, a magazine for people with arthritis.

Chapter 29
Two Songbirds

Jane Powell

I had the pleasure of meeting with Jane Powell a couple of times in preparation for writing articles that were never published.

In 1977, while still writing for *Coronet* and *In The Know,* I drove to her hilltop home in the tree-shaded canyons of Bel Air on assignment for the former.

During my visit, the petite (5', 90 lb.) blue-eyed blond told me she had owned the house for three years, but had not been able to spend much time there due to her live theatre work.

She served me a piece her own homemade chocolate cake and ,talked about her many house plants and a favorite view she enjoyed. Through the rear living room window, beyond her flower-bordered patio and swimming pool, one could see the blue waters of a reservoir surrounded by hills, with mountains taking over in the distance.

"I've never had a view before," she said. "Now, I sit and watch the lake change color as the day lengthens and the birds come in and I think it's a really beautiful place."

At that time, Jane was separated from her third husband, Jim

Fitzgerald. The mother of three children – Geary, Suzanne, and Lindsay – by her first two husbands, ice skater Geary Steffen and Patrick Nerney, she had arranged her schedule so as to provide them with an at-home mom as much as possible during their childhood years, turning down many professional offers with that in mind. But now they were grown up and out in the world on their own, so her favored companions were her two toy poodles, December and Dickens.

She told me that she had a singing teacher and that she practiced at least an hour every day. "I get tired of hearing myself sing," she admitted.

Of her many movies, I told her that my favorite was *Seven Brides for Seven Brothers*. She said that it had been a high point in her life, since it was so popular and considered an international favorite.

Unfortunately, although I completed my article about her, *Coronet* magazine (and *In The Know*, as well) closed down unexpectedly before it could see publication.

A few months later, when Jane was booked to star in a production of *South Pacific* at the Hollywood Pantages Theatre, I met with her again and wrote another article, this time for the *Los Angeles Times Calendar* section.

Our second interview was conducted over lunch at Warner Bros. Studios during a break from the *Fantasy Island* television series, in which Jane was appearing as a guest star. Before eating, I had the fun of visiting the set and making a brief acquaintance of its star, Fernando Lamas.

Jane was enjoying working with Howard Keel in *South Pacific* as he had been her *Seven Brides for Seven Brothers* co-star. She particularly liked the opportunity of being home in Los Angeles for that three week live theatre engagement.

Again, I turned in a completed article, but this one was rejected with a kill-fee. Although the editor claimed it was because I had written too much of a "puff-piece" about her, I was told by a higher-up that it was really because he considered *South Pacific* "too racist," and did not wish to publicize it. That was the first time I had encountered the problem of being considered "politically incorrect."

Carol Lawrence

My other "songbird" interview was to occur several years later with actress Carol Lawrence, who was most often associated with musical theatre, although she also did guest appearances on a number of TV series, including *The Golden Girls*. The assignment was for *The Franklin Mint Almanac*, and Ralph accompanied me to her two-story French Regency style home in Beverly Hills.

Born in Illinois, Carol had originally been named Carolina Maria Laraia. Her second husband had been singer Robert Goulet, and he was the father of her two grownup sons – Christopher and Michael.

Because I had become aware that my former schoolmate, Larry Kert , had co-starred with Carol in the Broadway production of *West Side Story*, I'd been eager to meet her. We talked about him a little, but since I have never visited New York City, I had never seen the show, just purchased its recording through a record club.

Carol had a number of interesting collectibles that she was to share with us for our article. The house, itself, proved to have its own fascination. Once the home of actress Kay Frances, it had a dining room lined with hand-painted mirrors which were the creation of set designer Don Loper, who had prevailed upon Carol to promise him that she would never "desecrate" the room with electric light fixtures. To that day, the mirrors reflected only candlelight dinners.

Carol's collections included Dresden figurines, lustrous ivory-colored Belleek (Irish porcelain) Items, and paintings by American watercolorist Ruth Cobb. There were 50 delicate curios made from actual eggs, and she had furnished her home with French and Italian antique furniture.

My favorite of her collections was one of antique clothing irons, many of which had elaborate decorations on them. They included small sadirons for children's clothing, slender sleeve irons, "crimpers" and "fluters" for ironing ruffles, and "self heating" box irons made to hold hot coals, metal slugs or charcoal bricks. Some irons weighed as much as fourteen pounds.

Her 1840 custom-made nine-foot-long rosewood Steinway grand piano was so huge that she had had to enlarge her living room to accommodate it. She had learned of its existence from the wife of Jonathan Winters, who had seen it in the store where she purchased her own French walnut baby grand.

An avid shopper on her world-wide travels as well as at local yard sales, Carol had stories to tell about many of her purchases

One of her favorite items was what she referred to as "a wonderful old puppet" of Rigoletto – from the Verde opera -- which she discovered in an antique shop in Paris.

Advised about bargaining techniques to be used with the French by her knowledgeable hairdresser, Carol had been told to act as if she were going to leave if she thought the price was too high. She was dismayed when the shopkeeper let her walk right out the door after quoting it as $200.

Because Carol really wanted the puppet, she went back again, but that time was told that the puppet was not for sale.

"This really shocked me," said Carol. "I quickly answered, 'Last week you told me it was $200.' She looked me in the eye and replied evenly, 'If I said $200, I can't go back on my word.'

Carol laughed hilariously. "She got the better of me. I didn't get her to lower the price as I'd hoped to do, but I bought it anyway, because I had to have it."

Chapter 30

Stars in the Sky

Pappy Boyington

When Ralph and I were given an assignment by *Collectibles Illustrated* magazine to do an article on the Air Museum in Chino, California, an added treat was meeting retired United States Marine flyer Colonel Gregory "Pappy" Boyington, who happened to be there that day autographing his recent book.

Pappy was best known during World War II as the organizer and leader of the off-beat Black Sheep squadron in the South Pacific. In the 1930s, he had attained the rank of lieutenant as a pilot in the Marines, then resigned his commission to join what was known as the "Flying Tigers," the American Volunteer Group, which was assisting the Republic of China Air Force in the Second Sino-Japanese War. After returning to the United States Marines during World War II, he joined a squadron of pilots unwanted by other outfits and guided and inspired them to deeds of valor. Its "Black Sheep" nickname was a mark of respect.

Flying Curtiss P-40 fighters painted with shark faces, he claimed to have shot down six of the Japanese I-97 planes while in the Flying Tigers, and scored the rest of his 28 victories in war battles with Japanese Zeros.

At the age of 31, he had been older than the other Marine fighter pilots by several years, so had been dubbed "Grandpappy," a name that was shortened to "Pappy."

Pappy was eventually shot down himself and spent about 20 months as a Japanese prisoner of war. He was awarded a Medal of Honor and a Navy Cross.

John Wayne had played him in the *Flying Tigers* movie, and, more recently, a TV series entitled *Baa Baa Black Sheep* had been based on his exploits.

Then in his 70s, Pappy was still performing in air shows.

Among other experiences he told me about was the first time he ever saw an airplane.

"It was in 1918 in the little town of Saint Maries, Idaho, where I lived then. I ran away from First Grade at recess. The teacher was screaming at me to come back and I told her, 'Nope, I gotta go down and get a ride in that airplane.' So I did, and the pilot was a freckle-faced young teenager who turned out to be one of your all-time aviation pioneers – a guy named Clyde Pangborn. He had me throwing out handbills. I wasn't at all scared. I had no shoes on and no goggles or helmet. I had to stand up to drop the papers out one at a time. The plane's engine was cooled with water, so globs of water and an occasional blob of oil would fly back and hit me in the face."

He grinned in remembrance. "The way I was perched in that open plane, it was a wonder I didn't hit a little air pocket and land in my mother's backyard."

Cliff Robertson

Driving onto the far-reaching stretches of a small California airport popular with the owners of private planes, Ralph and I were dismayed to see Cliff Robertson taking off in his modern Beech Baron. Although our appointment to discuss his airplane collection was now, we reasoned that the busy actor had not been able to resist the skies on this gorgeous balmy day.

We watched the cream-colored aircraft fade to a speck over a distant purple foothill, breathing sighs of acceptance.

But when he returned, we found ourselves dealing with yet more interruptions. The first was when he flew off yet again to comply with someone else's request to photograph him flying his French Stampe biplane. And then there were all his cronies who wandered over from neighboring hangars.

"I designed and built this double hangar about 25 years ago," Cliff told us when we finally got him to sit down and talk.

Large enough to hold half a dozen small aircraft, it was the homeport for his three British Tiger Moths, the Stampe, and his twin-engined Beech Baron, which he used for cross-country flights and location scouting. His British "Spitfire" and German Messerschmitt were kept elsewhere.

A licensed commercial pilot, Cliff told us about acquiring his interest in airplanes at an early age.

"In the summertime I used to pedal my bicycle to a little dirt airport near my home in La Jolla that no longer exists. When I was about 14, I would work eight hours a day, with no pay, cleaning all the dirty parts of the plane engines. About every third day, they'd let me go up for around 10 minutes in a Taylor Cub for free and give me a little flying instruction. I thought I was the luckiest guy in the world."

First a journalist, then deciding to be a playwright, he became sidetracked with a professional acting job in the New York Catskills. He joined the Actor's Studio, trained, and appeared in various off-Broadway productions. His film debut was in *Picnic* and he was chosen by President John Kennedy for the lead in *PT 109*, the president's own story of his wartime adventures.

A few of his long-list of movie and television roles were *Charly* (which he purchased, re-wrote, starred in and received the Academy Award for Best Actor), *The Naked and the Dead*, *My Six Loves*, *Gidget*, *Brainstorm*, and *Star 80*. Particularly appropriate roles were *The Pilot* and Astronaut Buzz Aldrin in *Return To Earth*.

Cliff said he was finishing a movie in England when he decided to buy his first airplane.

"I was going over to do another movie in France and I thought it would be nice to fly at the end of the day when there was still a little sun left. I put an ad in the paper and bought a Tiger Moth and named it Annie. It's the only plane to which I've ever given a name."

He told us he bought his second Tiger Moth from an Air Force base in the Philippines for extra parts, but found it too good to tear down.

"Some years later, I bought a third, again thinking I'd have parts, but it turned out to be as good as the other two. So I ended up with three Tiger Moths, but they are not a luxury. I put them all to work for movies and television."

Chapter 31

Four Young Ladies

Ralph and I did several brief interview sessions with people who were in the public eye largely due to their current or recent television roles. These four were some of them.

Courtney Cox

At the time when we visited the Los Angeles area canyon home of Courtney Cox, she was still portraying Lauren Miller, the love interest of Alex Keaton played by Michael J. Fox on the *Family Ties* TV series.

Earlier, the former Ford teenage model had played a delinquent teenager in the NBC series *Misfits of Science*.

When we spotted a set of drums in her living room and asked her about it, she told us they really were hers.

"I played an Earthling girl in the movie *Masters of the Universe*," she said. "When the film was finished, I got the set of drums they had used on the music shop set. My stepfather's nephew is Stewart Copeland of *The Police* and he taught me the basics. I also play the guitar."

She laughed when we asked her about the tabloid rumor of a

romance between her and her *Family Ties* co-star. "It's not true at all," she insisted. "We've never even dated. He has a girl friend and I have a boy friend."

Diane Kay

We learned some unusual things about Diane Kay, who was known as Nancy Bradford on the *Eight Is Enough* television series.

The first was that she collected soft-sculpture dolls which were created in the image of famous people. They were made by an artist named David Strauss,

"I have W.C. Fields, Oliver Hardy, Humphrey Bogart, Charlie Chaplin, Mae West, Greta Garbo, Groucho Marx, Fred Astaire, and Judy Garland," she said, indicating each one as she said the names.

She also told us about what she considered psychic happenings that she had experienced during her life.

"I had an out-of-body experience at the age of three," she began.

"Some grownups attending a party my parents were giving asked me how old I was. I told them and held up three fingers. All of a sudden, I felt outside my body and above them. Looking down, I saw this little child holding up three fingers and the big people looking at her. I was laughing to myself and thinking, 'Isn't this funny? I'm bigger than the big people and they don't even know.'"

She also told about an episode of participating in "automatic writing" as a teenager when she found herself writing words of wisdom she didn't know but that came into her mind.

"When I told a friend, she said I had somehow made contact with an entity who wanted to tell me something and that I was open to it, on a wavelength like a transistor radio."

Tori Spelling

Ralph and I found ourselves interviewing two well-known 21-year-olds on the day we visited a certain high-rise co-op apartment in a snooty Beverly Hills neighborhood. Tori Spelling and Nicholas Savalas were both there.

Asking Tori what first attracted her about Nicholas, middle son of the by then late actor Telly Savalas, when they had met two years before, she said, in her soft little voice, "I don't know."

"You have to think of something," Nick urged her gently.

Tori made an effort. "He was cute, I guess."

Same question put to Nick, regarding Tori.

His answer, "I don't know."

When pressed, Tori continued, if reluctantly, "He's really very funny and he's very charming."

People supposedly in the know had told us that they would probably marry sometime in the future, but that, at the moment, they were both too busy with their careers.

For the present, Tori was involved with the *Beverly Hills 90210* series. She had known since the age of five that she wanted to act, had been taking acting classes, and been given "little spots" in her dad's shows from then on.

Nick, who had been referred to as "a young Marlon Brando type," resembled his late father. Though interested in semi-pro tennis, he had opted for acting and begun taking acting classes, too

The apartment resounded with the raucous voice of Charley, the female parrot, which the couple had brought back from a trip to Hawaii.

I later learned that their marriage never did take place.

Lauren Tewes

In my opinion, the television series *The Love Boat* would not have been quite so appealing in its beginning had it not had Lauren Tewes (pronounced tweeze) portraying perky cruise director Julie McCoy.

But, by the time Ralph and I connected with her, she had been to and was back from what she referred to as "Cocaine Hell." After being given some at a party, she had become addicted, was fired from her cushy television role, and later recovered.

On this day, she had met with us by the outer wall of the Paramount Studios to talk a bit and be photographed for an article. The reason for public interest in her at that time was that she had been invited to return for the show's tenth season. Apparently that was because when she had been a guest star on that show the previous fall, it had resulted in being the highest rated episode of 1985.

"I got an awful lot of very personal mail when I left *The Love Boat*," she explained. "It was from people saying, 'I miss you and I hope you're well and happy.'"

Lauren credited the children's television star Mr. Rogers with being her inspiration to conquer her drug addiction.

"I was alone when I woke up and heard him asking, 'Will you be my friend?' I realized that I really needed a friend, and I said, 'Yes.' I resolved to get my act together. I didn't stop taking Cocaine overnight – just little by little, but finally, I was able to quit completely."

Later, she met that gentleman while both were appearing on a talk show and told him of her experience.

"He said it meant a lot to him and he realized his show reached a lot of people and not just children under 10. He gave me a tee-shirt, which I still have."

She smiled thoughtfully. "What a good, kind man. I would never make fun of Mr. Rogers. He helped me too much."

Chapter 32

Plain Jane, Not Doctor Quinn

My interview with Jane Seymour happened in 1986 – several years before the lovely, long-haired lady even thought of becoming *Dr. Quinn, Medicine Woman*. And long before she became the mother of twins. My subsequent article appeared in *Sunday Woman Plus*, a Sunday supplement connected with a number of newspapers.

At that time, married to her fourth husband, David Flynn, a Hollywood business manager, Jane was full of stories about the special parties and activities she instigated for their four-year-old daughter Katie and her younger brother, Sean Michael. She told me in detail about the Chuck E Cheese gala when she asked each young guest to wear white or grey, then added string tails and had their faces painted white with whiskers.

Her book, entitled *Jane Seymour's Guide to Romantic Living*, was about to be made available in bookstores and she was eager to talk about it.

"Making movies is fun. It's exciting and it's my job," she proclaimed. "But writing is my passion. I'd never written so much as an essay before, but it's an idea I've had for a long time. It's part of my life. I'm deemed an eccentric to a certain extent by my friends and my family, although my family is just as eccentric as I am."

We'd met that day for the first time in the large living room of her Beverly Hills home. Jane sat opposite me on a boxy white couch, her gleaming brown tresses spreading out over the shoulders of a deep cobalt blue dress decorated with a rhinestone-encrusted cherub pin backed by large green leaves shaped like wings. She decided to try explaining herself to me.

"When I get up in the morning — if I'm not acting another role — I don't know who I'm going to be that day," she began in her beautifully modulated voice. "Am I going to be a lady in white or a lady in blue? Am I going to be a little vampy or do I feel like being angelic?"

She smiled benignly. "Trust me, I don't spend more than ten or fifteen minutes deciding. I mean it's whatever first hits my fancy in the wardrobe. Then, of course, I'm awfully practical. I'll wear something twice because it has to go to the cleaners. But I'll make it look different the second wearing.

"This is a very old dress," she continued earnestly, " at least four or five years old. I never throw stuff out." She told me that to dramatize the outfit today she'd added a rhinestone covered leather cowboy belt made by a friend and high-heeled boots she'd found in Italy.

Determined to clue me in about what she considered "romantic living," she said, "It means bringing suspense, adventure, excitement and drama – femininity for women and chivalry for men – into your life. In other words, don't feel obliged to give somebody a present on Valentine's Day because Hallmark Cards tells you that you have to. Give it ten days before because you feel like it. And surprise that person. Don't be afraid to do something different. Instead of sitting inside on a rainy day, go out and walk in the rain. Positive people attract other positive people and when you're negative, you get nothing but misery, and people avoid you in droves."

Born Joyce Penelope Wilhelmina Frankenberg in Middlesex, England, Jane said she'd studied ballet from the age of two and might have become a prima ballerina if she hadn't injured her knee.

At 16, she decided to become an actress and took for her stage name that of one of Henry VIII's six wives. She appeared in movie, radio, and television roles including the six-hour TV version of *Far From the Madding Crowd, Young Winston, Solitaire* and the 007 movie, *Live and Let Die.*

Once in Hollywood, she was encouraged to "lose her English accent," so settled into a comfortable Middle Atlantic dialect. *Battlestar Galactica* and *Somewhere in Time,* co-starring Christopher Reeves were some of her films.

At the time of our interview, she was preparing to go to Poland to face the grim head-shaving scene for *War and Remembrance* – the 30-hour mini-series sequel to the 18-hour *Winds of War.*

Planning a reunion with her parents in Auschwitch, she told me a bit of what she termed "wonderful things" they had done with their children.

"We didn't have money for glamorous holidays, but, with my two sisters and I, they would get into our very old car with maps and we'd follow the Rhine or follow the Danube until we found a special place to stop and have a picnic. We might tour a castle or buy frankfurters in Frankfurt or cheese in France. It was always an adventure."

Always original, Jane said that the jewel she wore in her hair for the dust jacket photo on her book was not actually a tiara, but an earring. "The ornament at my throat was the rather elaborate clasp of a long string of pearls I put on backwards for the picture session. If I'd turned around, you'd have seen the pearls hanging down my back."

Returning to the subject of romantic living, Jane gave me another example: It happened on the opening night of her Broadway production of *Amadeus*, for which she'd originated the role of Constanze Weber, wife of Mozart.

"The whole world had given me flowers," she gushed, "but there was nothing from my husband.

I'm feeling kind of hurt and disappointed and the curtain is about to go up any second. Then, suddenly, the door of my tiny dressing room is flung open and three dozen red roses are strewn all over the room. 'Here are your flowers, darling. Good luck.' He just threw the flowers and ran. That," she finished proudly, "is my husband."

But life with that husband must have eventually turned out to be a disappointment after all. Her eleven year marriage to David Flynn was to end in divorce in 1992.

It was followed by her marriage to James Keach and the birth of their twin sons, Johnny and Kris – named for family friends, Johnny Cash and Christopher Reeves.

Jane was to star in *Dr. Quinn, Medicine Woman* during the1990s. On New Year's Eve, 1999, she was named an Officer of the Order of the British Empire by Queen Elizabeth. And in 2005 she became a naturalized American citizen. She is a celebrity ambassador for the Childhelp organization.

Chapter 33

I Say Hello to Dolly Parton

At a two-day writer's conference in San Diego, I had met an editor for a Sunday supplement entitled *Northeast Woman* and was pleasantly surprised to receive a phone call asking me to take over an interview with Dolly Parton because the already assigned writer had broken her shoulder.

Because my time was too limited to receive biographical research material, I ran out and bought a couple of paperback books about her. But, books aside, I was to learn that Dolly Parton was a very natural, friendly, and considerate person. And, though it never happened, I was to wish that I could have had more chances to meet with her.

I parked in the lot of the Beverly Hills Hotel and walked around to the proper bungalow.

Dolly's publicist met me at the door and, as soon as I entered, Dolly burst like sunlight into the living room and settled herself on the small couch.

She looked slim and trim in a red-and-white zig-zaggy patterned sweater over fitted tan pants that were partially covered by calf-high custom-made red high-heeled boots. Her saucy blond hairdo, which might have been one of her many wigs, was exactly as I expected.

The occasion for her being in town was a "comeback" after recovering from a series of physical difficulties including bleeding ulcers and gynecological and digestive problems.

I chose to sit on a large bulky stool to be near enough for my mini tape recorder to catch what she said.

"I'm really happy to be back in good health and I feel more productive and better off than I've been all my life," she began cheerfully.

She'd enjoyed a brief vacation in Hawaii with her husband, Carl Dean -- following the making of her third movie, *Rhinestone* – during which the couple had purchased a new island home. She also had a new album called *The Great Pretender*.

Upcoming projects she listed for me included the writing of a Broadway musical called *Wildflower*, creating a production company for television shows and series as well as TV movies and regular movies, a line of clothing and another of cosmetics she planned to offer. As far as the clothes went, her idea was to include "clothes for heavy, hefty, shorter people," because she recalled having a hard time finding clothes for herself, "being little and big-busted and big in the hips.

"When I was just a real young girl I was impressed with what they called the 'trash' in our hometown. They were the women that wore the lipstick and had blond hair. I was a blond when I was a kid and my hair started to get a dirtier blond when I reached my teens, so I started bleaching it when I was about fifteen. That was about the time that 'teasing' came out and that was something real creative to do so I got real good at that." She grinned. "I had hair piled high as everything. I liked tight clothes and high-heeled shoes and I just kind of created a 'look.'"

She told me that her 'look' also had some of the over-exaggerated glamour of the sort of clothing of fairytale queens, fairy godmothers and Mother Goose. And that it included her wigs.

"I really enjoy wearing my wigs, because to me it's just like something fun to play in. I keep my own hair blond by bleaching it every ten days, but it's straight and baby-fine and it just will not do what I want it to do. So the wigs are wonderful and handy."

We talked for quite a while about many things including her husband, whom Dolly said was so rarely seen by the show business crowd that she had actually been accused of making him up as a means of fending off unwanted suitors.

She laughed heartily. "I even get to thinking it myself. Sometimes I say to people, 'Well, that's true, I have a rent-a-husband. I have a guy or even a few guys, so if I want to go out and say 'This is my husband, Carl Dean.' It's a name I made up.' And they say, 'I *know* there's no Carl Dean. I *know* you don't have a husband.'"

The truth is that she made an agreement with him many years ago that he would not have to be a part of her professional life.

She told me that even though she was branching out in other directions, her first love – music – was usually involved in some way.

"Coming from the backwoods, there was no other way for me to start out except in country and folk music. I was very, very country. Now I can sing in almost any style. I can travel all over and I love that," she said.

And then she said the words that I was to use in the title of my article: *Dolly Parton, Blond But Not Vanilla.*

"I don't want people to think that I'm perfect. I don't want to be vanilla. I'd rather be chocolate ripple or rocky road. I'm not a goody-goody. I want to be a good person, but not a goody-goody. I used to feel guilty about some of the things I did, thinking that they went against the way I had been brought up to believe, but then I realized there wasn't anything coming out of my guilt but self destruction. I came to terms with myself and with my God as I know Him. If I am doing things that make me happy, by my own joy other people can see that joy and be touched by it. Otherwise, I'd just be a lost cause."

Among the many charitable projects Dolly had accomplished at that time were her annual performances in her hometown of Sevierville, Tennessee, from which proceeds went to the local high school and its special scholarship fund for students.

I asked Dolly if she would sing a song for me and she readily agreed. My choice was "Jolene," and I really enjoyed it when she obliged me.

It was time for me to go, and Dolly followed me to the door to let me out.

As we started to say our goodbyes, she surprised me by asking suddenly and kindly, "Do you have to pee or anything before you go?"

Taken off guard, I answered "No, thanks."

However, as soon as I was back in my car, I regretted not taking her up on the offer. I had a long drive home on the freeway ahead of me.

Chapter 34

The Beauty of Being Brittany

Morgan Brittany was another of the people Ralph and I had more than one occasion to visit. But, actually, I first met her on assignment to *Woman's World* along with Steve Shapiro, the photographer they had hired to do the job.

Although my cover story was an at-home style double page spread, the slant was geared toward her so-called "keys to beauty."

The year was 1986 and the beautiful dark-auburn-haired actress was living in a pleasant three bedroom ranch-style house overlooking the west San Fernando Valley with her husband, stuntman Jack Gill, her baby daughter Katie, and their two dogs.

At that time she was co-host with Bruce Jenner of TV's *Star Games* and was best known for playing Katherine Wentworth, the one who shot Bobby Ewing (Patrick Duffy) on the TV series *Dallas*.

I spent a relaxing time exploring her cozy home with its Victorian and art deco antiques, watching her work out on the gym equipment housed above her garage, and talking with Morgan about her thoughts on beauty. "Think beautiful thoughts and they'll be reflected in your looks," I recall her saying. And she also believed it was important for a woman to feel good about herself.

By the time Ralph and I learned about Morgan's doll collection, *Collectibles Illustrated* had closed down, as had *The Franklin Mint Almanac*. However, the Franklin Mint was publishing an attractive slick-paged *Doll Collector* "newsletter."

And also, by this time, Morgan and Jack were living further out on an impressive hillside house in the Agoura Hills area.

We drove out and spent a few hours learning about and photographing Morgan with some of her fascinating "finds."

She was especially fond of the Franklin Mint *Gone With the Wind* collector dolls, because during her career she had had the opportunity to portray Scarlett O'Hara and Vivien Leigh, the original Scarlett O'Hara actress who played that role in the 1939 movie version of *Gone With the Wind*.

"In *The Day of the Locust*, as her 'look-a-like,' I was in a big Hollywood premiere scene playing Vivien Leigh. In *Gable and Lombard*, we did Vivien's Atlanta scene. And in *Moviola*, I played Vivien Leigh as she was being discovered for the role of Scarlett. Before those movies, I had already played Scarlett in a couple of television commercials," she told us.

She had about 150 dolls, including a German-made Simon and Halvig doll she thought resembled Bonnie Blue Butler, the daughter of Scarlett and Rhett. Another special doll was an 1880's French Jules Steiner one with blown-glass eyes. And she was having a Victorian dollhouse restored.

Another of our Morgan Brittany stories – written as a side feature for an arthritis magazine -- dealt with her passion for romance novels.

She told us how she first became interested in reading that type of book during her teenage years.

Born Suzanne Cupito, she had been a child actress since the age of five, beginning with a role on an episode of the TV series *Sea Hunt*, starring Lloyd Bridges. In the movie version of *Gypsy*, she played the youngest "Baby June," and was one of the frightened school children in the movie *The Birds*. Then, as a teenager, she played a daughter of Lucille Ball and Henry Fonda in *Yours, Mine and Ours*.

"I took refuge in romance novels in my early teens because I felt unattractive and unwanted in my own life. I felt like a has-been" she said.

"My family hails from Atlanta, Georgia and my mother has always been a collector of historical novels pertaining to the South. My favorite book of all time is *Gone With the Wind*."

She said she "absolutely adored" *Wuthering Heights* by Emily Brontë, calling it "a hauntingly romantic ghost story" and also enjoyed *Jane Eyre*, written by her sister Charlotte, both published in the nineteenth century.

"*Tap Roots*, by J. H. Street, another Southern novel I particularly liked, was made into a movie starring Susan Hayward and Van Heflin," she said.

She talked about Frank Yerby – the first African American to write a best-selling novel. (He was born in Augusta, Georgia in 1916 to a Scotts-Irish mother and a black father.)

"Some people might not agree with me calling Frank Yerby a romance novelist, but that is what he seems to me. His stories are very romantic and I like the fact that his women characters are strong and notable people. His novel *The Foxes of Harrow* was made into a movie in 1947 with Rex Harrison and Maureen O'Hara. Other of his novels I've read are *Bride of Liberty*, *Fairoaks*, *A Woman Called Fancy*, *Griffin's Way*, *Jarrett's Jade* and *Goat Song*."

*S*he told us the story of how she "became" Morgan Brittany.

"It came about because I wanted to go into modeling and had been told by a Los Angeles agent that I wasn't the right type. I decided to give New York a try. En route by plane, I was reading a Frank Yerby novel entitled *Floodtide* when I got the idea of changing my name. I reasoned that it would give me a fresh start. But what should I call myself?

"My eye lit upon a page of the book where one unusual name stood out. Morgan Brittany. She was a major character, though not a particularly nice one. (When I played Katherine Wentworth on *Dallas* about 10 years later, I saw a striking resemblance to her.) But she certainly wasn't a woman to be ignored. The wife of a planter named Lance Brittany in the story, she was the kind who could cast a spell over any man and she did. She commissioned a young architect to build the finest plantation in the South and she was having an affair with him. I didn't exactly admire the character, but I loved the name. So it was Morgan Brittany who got off that plane in New York, wearing my face.

"Whether or not the new name had anything to do with it, I'm not certain, but things began to improve. Within a month I had six national commercial spots and was asked to represent a Japanese cosmetics firm. I was working for them when the call came to do the Vivien Leigh part."

She thought a moment; then continued.

"I've often wondered if Frank Yerby ever heard about me and realized I had adopted the name of one of his characters."

Chapter 35
The Musicians

Over the years of my celebrity interviews, I met and wrote articles about a few famous people in the music business. This chapter will tell what I learned about some of those people.

Horace Heidt

This gentleman was in his 80s by the time Ralph and I visited his San Fernando Valley home and museum. Once known as the HH Ranch – the center of an executive network, training farm, studio, and temporary living quarters for young performers, the property was then an attractive, well landscaped 170 unit apartment complex presided over by Heidt himself as manager.

The museum, which was attached to Mr. Heidt's own living quarters, was a nearly 3,000 square foot hall of mementoes of the career of pianist/composer/big band leader Horace Heidt and His Musical Knights.

Created by combining the former rehearsal hall, a trophy room, and additional footage, the museum included one particularly unusual feature. An open cellar door led down to a bomb shelter unit built in 1941 and originally reached by a road that was also included as part of the room.

Born in Alameda, California in 1901, Heidt had played football while attending the University of California and intended to turn pro. However, a broken back injury caused him to change his mind. During his recovery, he listened to Guy Lombardo on the radio, formed a five piece band in 1923, and performed at the Claremont Hotel in Berkeley.

"We billed ourselves as The World's Greatest Orchestra," he said, "but nobody believed it but us."

When the hotel was sold, the orchestra quit, and Heidt had to start all over again.

He did, however, become the leader of a very popular dance band and his performing days encompassed the Golden Age of Radio and pioneering days of television. Two of his memorable compositions are "I Don't Want To Set The World On Fire," and "The Hut Sut Song." His son, Horace, Jr has followed in his footsteps.

David Rose

Ralph and I visited the Sherman Oaks home of David Rose, who, then in his 70s, was known for composing, conducting, and arranging about 5,000 hours of music, recording more than 50 albums, scoring 36 films and creating background music and themes for 24 television series including *Bonanza* and *Little House on the Prairie*.

However, I really don't have a lot to say about him as our purpose in going there was to observe and write about his collection of miniature trains, with working steam engines, which circled his large yard. For some reason, the trains were not prepared to operate at that time so we never really completed our project.

The only thing I came away with, that I hadn't known before, was that Mr. Rose had composed "Holiday for Strings" and the recognizable tune known as "The Stripper", which generally indicates when a person of that occupation is about to perform.

Buddy Rich

I'm not embarrassed to admit that I had never heard of the famous drummer, Buddy Rich, until I received an assignment to write an "as-told-to" article about him. Knowing a lot about individual musicians just wasn't my kind of thing.

I was to learn that he had been born Bernard Rich in Brooklyn in 1917 and, as his bio told me, had kept noted Jazz bands swinging for over 50 years. It was said that he'd been called "the most brilliant and dynamic drummer of all time," And, at that time he was still heading his own band, which he termed "the best band in the country today."

As it turned out, I have reason to believe that I may well have been the last person to enjoy the privilege of interviewing that very talented gentleman for a major story. The reason? Mr. Rich passed away within days after our talk and even before my article was published in the Arthritis Information Magazine, *AIM PLUS*. But, published it was, as it was too late for the editors to cancel.

Ralph and I met with Buddy in a large park in the Century City area of Los Angeles.

An as-told-to article is one which is written in the first person as though the interviewee is telling his own story.

Buddy told me that, because his father was a combination comic and singer and dancer, and his mother a singer, he had been put on a stage before an audience at the age of two. By the time he was three, he was known as Baby Traps.

"I played the drums and tap-danced on Broadway," he recalled. "Nobody knows how I learned to play them, but for as long as I can remember, I had my own set of drums. By the time I was seven-years-old, I'd already been in two Broadway shows and traveled around the world. When I was 11-years-old, I was put in front of a Big Band. It was really just an act. Over the years I played drums with a bunch of guys. It was part of my youth, my growing up and learning."

John Tesh

In 1994, I wrote two separate stories regarding John Tesh that were both published in *Woman's World* magazine within just a couple of months. The first was about the new baby girl named Prima that he and his wife Connie Sellecca had welcomed into their lives in June of that year. The second was a Question-and-Answer (Q&A) article.

I met with the handsome 6'6" tall host of the *Entertainment Tonight* television show at NBC Studio.

A talented pianist and composer, he told me that he began playing the piano at the age of six and trained at Julliard School of Music. By then, he had nine albums to his credit and was about to release yet a tenth, entitled *Family Christmas*. He had also composed theme songs for a number of TV productions.

Much of our conversation centered around his new baby daughter.

"Prima was named for her maternal grandfather, Primo Sell-ecchia," John said. "She has big hands for a baby, so she might be good at the piano. And music ability does run in my family."

And he also talked enthusiastically about his 13-year-old stepson, Connie's son by her former husband, Gil Gerard.

"Gib is a brilliant pianist with perfect pitch, but he's not partic-ularly interested in it," he admitted. But he smiled when he added that "He is very protective of his baby sister."

Chapter 36

Thanks to Florence Henderson

It was thanks to Florence Henderson that Ralph and I became connected with another magazine that was to purchase celebrity cover stories from us on a regular monthly basis for the following several years, until it closed down.

I had known Florence since the late 1970s when I met and wrote about her through the Kroffts, who were responsible for producing a follow-up series to *The Brady Bunch*, entitled *The Brady Bunch Hour*. I had also written a story for *Westways* magazine about her former husband, Theatrical Producer Ira Bernstein, and his collection of toy cars.

Some years later, on returning home from a week's sojourn on an Alaskan cruise, I found a message on my answering machine that was a pleasant surprise. It was from the editor of *Mature American* magazine, a publication I had never heard of, telling me that they wanted a cover story on Florence Henderson. Apparently, they had already requested an interview with Florence, but she had told them that she wanted me to do the story and that they should contact me.

I shall always be grateful to that lovely lady for being so generous and thoughtful as to present me with that career enhancing opportunity.

By this time, Florence was divorced from her first husband (the father of her four grown children) and had married Dr. John Kappas, retired director of a San Fernando Valley hypnotherapy college and clinic.

The couple was living on their seventy foot motor yacht anchored at a Los Angeles area marina and it was considered a great privilege for us to conduct our interview and photo session in that very private locale.

I found it to be a delightful setting. In fact, listening to Florence tell us about the relaxing benefits of the negative ions one encounters with the fresh salt air when being near the ocean, made me both glad to be there and envious of her for that ongoing opportunity.

"Living on a boat simplifies your life so you aren't bogged down with possessions," Florence said. But she was also quick to admit that, as a performer needing an extensive wardrobe, she had filled five closets aboard ship, including one entire room which had been turned into a walk-in one. (And she also had storage space at a land location.)

I already knew about Florence's early background.

She was the youngest child of a close-knit "sharecropping" family of 10 children growing up in Kentucky and had learned what it was to work at an early age. By the time she was eight, she had spent long hours earning wages in the homes of others by such tasks as washing, ironing, cleaning house, cooking, and taking care of younger children. By the age of two, she knew the words to approximately 50 different songs and was often called upon to "entertain" her other family members.

Later, she attended The New York Academy of Dramatic Arts and eventually won the lead in the last national company of *Oklahoma!*. She made a movie, *The Song of Norway*, in 1970, right before beginning *The Brady Bunch*.

Recently, she had appeared in a *Murder, She Wrote* episode and was involved with her own cable cooking show called *Country Kitchen*, which she hosted regularly in Nashville. In keeping with that topic was the book she wrote entitled *A Little Cooking, A Little Talking, And a Whole Lot of Fun*. And she had a video telling some of her personal secrets for *Looking Good, Feeling Good*.

Since cooking was never a favorite activity for her, she had been somewhat reluctant to accept that format for her talk show. But they told her that her guests would do the cooking. They had included Willie Nelson, Minnie Pearl, Robert Reed, Rosie Grier, Phyllis Diller, Mel Tillis, Jim Nabors, Barbara Eden, Jimmy Dean and her Brady "son," Barry Williams.

Florence told me about meeting her current husband.

She said that, although she had never before suffered from stage fright, she had all of a sudden been stricken with that problem. To remedy it, she underwent hypnotherapy, during which she met John. She found herself not only cured, but so impressed with the process that she went on to become a clinical hypnotherapist herself and had actually helped other people with a variety of problems.

And, of course, she also proceeded to marry John.

She explained that, when her busy schedule allowed, they enjoyed untying their boat and paying visits to such other nearby ports as Catalina, Newport, or San Diego. They also had hopes of undertaking a voyage to Alaska someday.

In the meantime, however, "Just coming home to the boat is like being on vacation," Florence said with a smile.

In keeping with our habit of staying in touch with many of the people we interviewed, not long after this, Ralph and I did another story on Florence for a health magazine.

Chapter 37

Anne Francis – A Honey of a Gal

Anne Francis has sometimes been referred to as "the lovely blond with the beauty mark."

Because that feature definitely sets her apart, it was one of the things I asked her about when Ralph and I paid her a visit at her secluded Santa Barbara home.

Not at all reluctant to discuss it, she smiled and answered with the following remarks.

"It has both advantages and disadvantages. If you're going in for a character role, they're apt to remember you as the actress who played a glamorous one before, which is no help at all. There've been times when I did my best to cover up my mole.

"I once asked a dermatologist if he'd consider removing it, but he said, 'Are you kidding? That's part of who you are. There's no way I'm going to take that responsibility.'"

And even her personal friends have wondered if it was for real when a "flipped" picture caused it to appear on the other side of her face.

But, of course we had so many more things to talk about.

Bringing us up to date on her recent accomplishments, Anne told us that she had not been out and about career-wise for some time due to the fact that she had been serving as a caregiver for her mother, who had eventually passed on at the age of 94. "She was still driving a car when she was 90," she remarked.

We discussed the obvious projects that most people associated with her.

About *Forbidden Planet*, the 1956 science fiction film in which she had co-starred with Walter Pigeon , Leslie Nielson, and Robby the Robot, she said, "It was a challenge re-acting to a menace that really wasn't there, since the special effects, added later for the audience, were not in evidence to the actors."

Another favorite of mine had been *Bad Day at Black Rock*, which also starred Spencer Tracy and Robert Ryan. And *Blackboard Jungle* had co-starred my friend, Glenn Ford. About the latter, she reminded me that "*Blackboard Jungle* was the first film to feature rock music, with 'Rock Around the Clock' being played with its opening credits."

Anne's own 1965-66 Golden Globe Award-winning TV series *Honey West* had been termed "a fetching female James Bond," and made use of a number of spy gadgets such as a lipstick containing a transmitter radio.

Anne told us about her character's pet ocelot.

"His name was Bruce Bite-a-Bit, which certainly fit as that was what he did. As with a kitten, you never knew if he was happy or unhappy. When he was happy, he'd bite and scratch and when he was annoyed, he'd scratch and bite. So who knew? Working with him was like handling two cobras – each end seemed to be independent of the other. But I liked him. I love cats, so I thought he was beautiful and wonderful.

"I studied karate for a couple of months before the show," Anne told us. "I did a lot of my own stunt work like fight scenes and driving the Corvette up to the edge of a cliff and slamming on the brakes. When the director wanted me to jump from a truck into the street, wearing high heels and a tight fitting evening gown, however, I drew the line. I wasn't about to risk breaking an ankle."

Our conversation reminded her of a time when she did a love scene with Jim Drury on the TV series *The Virginian*.

"We were to share a passionate kiss in a doorway and there were to be gunshots whizzing by from someone who was after Jim. The special effects man installed slugs in the doorframe to create the explosions. I was a little concerned, but he said, 'Oh, they're just quarter loads, so there's no problem at all.'

"Well," she paused for effect. "We did the kiss and I got hit on the side of my face. Thank God it was the *side* of my face. I was blown clear across the sound stage and landed on the floor. I thought I had lost half of my face. I hadn't. It was just full of splinters from the doorframe. It turned out that it was a *full* load after all. It absolutely shattered my nervous system for the rest of the afternoon."

Over the years, Anne had done lots of live theater in both the United States and Canada, and she also wrote, directed, and produced an art film short, *Gemini Rising* – about a rodeo as seen through the eyes of a young boy. She is the author of an autobiographical book entitled *Voices from Home*, and won a first place award at the Santa Barbara Writers' Conference for film writing.

Although she had been married twice for comparatively brief

periods, she was unmarried at that time. She was mother to two daughters – Jane and Margaret (known as Maggie).

Since moving to Santa Barbara, Anne had been active in local charitable organizations as well as Direct Relief International, which sends medical supplies all over the world.

Because it was lunchtime by the time we finished talking and photographing Anne, she graciously drove us to a nearby favorite restaurant of mine in Montecito and treated us to a delicious meal.

Chapter 38

Angie Dickinson is One of a Kind

Thinking back to the times Ralph and I spent with Angie Dickinson, I've tried to recall what I thought about the popular, talented actress who was born with the same last name as I was – Brown. On the whole, I would say that I think of Angie as being a totally nice and generous person. But that is far too simple of a description. She deserves better, because she is much more complex than that implies.

First, let me set the stage by saying that all of our visits with Angie were held at the two story Mediterranean style house located in a secluded canyon near Beverly Hills which she had once shared with her second husband, composer/pianist Burt Bacharach.

The almost-acre was walled in and inviting with flowers and backyard shade trees that made me mentally compare her large swimming pool to a lake in the woods. I am pleased to say that she once offered me the privilege of coming down to use her pool whenever I might want to, although I never had the occasion to accept. Truly fond of a wide variety of flowers, Angie loved to garden and filled her rooms as well as her yard with flowering plants.

Words I used to describe her in some of the articles I had occasion to write about her included "unchanging," and "a perennial
beauty." I also wrote about her honey-soft voice and her honey-
blond hair and brown eyes.

I learned about her "fairness" when I wrote about her for a
tabloid publication, with her blessing. Although I had listened to
her tell about experiences with Bacharach, never once had I discussed or written about any of the other men in her life. Yet, when
the article appeared, someone had taken the liberty to add comments about the best known of those gentlemen.

Horrified, I phoned Angie to try to explain, telling her that I
had not included those comments in my original article. To Angie's credit, she believed me and absolved me from any blame.

"Did you get your money?" she asked calmly. And, when I replied that I had, she simply said, "Then don't worry about it."

Another side of Angie had to do with the television show
entitled *This Is Your Life*, which honored celebrities through biographical information and visits with people from their past.

About that I wrote the following in one of my articles:

One doesn't sneak up on Angie Dickinson – not even with
friendly intent.

When Ralph Edwards decided to pay tribute to the famous
actress, he made the mistake of tricking her into showing up – as
is his time-honored custom – by informing her that she would be
speaking up for another.

Angie's close associates should have been able to advise him
this was a "no-no."

To his complete astonishment, when Edwards uttered the
well-known phrase, "Angie Dickinson, this is your life," the horri-

fied Angie shot back, "No it isn't!" And, before he could blink his eyes, she had walked out the door.

A typical Libran (the astrological sign of the scales for her September 30th birthday), Dickinson needs time to ponder and weigh the pros and cons of any situation. She doesn't like to be rushed and she's not much on surprises.

In this case, she felt the need to apologize individually to all concerned in the "surprise," including Earl Holliman, her co-star in the *Police Woman* TV series, and Bob Hope, who reportedly had given up a dinner engagement with Nancy and Ronald Reagan to be present.

She also did her best to explain on TV news that her reluctance to be so honored might be relegated to "vanity. I would have been 'teary-eyed' when they brought out old friends and acquaintances."

But, to me (who was married to a Libran) this was just another proof that Miss Dickinson was truly a "one of a kind." individual.

Angie liked to say that she was very fond of Taurus men. This pleased Ralph, who himself is a Taurus. But her real Taurus favorite was Burt Bacharach and she told me the story of how they met.

While visiting New York, she had granted an interview to his father, Bert Bacharach, who was a writer. [The difference in the spelling of their first names is not an error.]

"He told me I should meet his son," she explained. "I didn't even know what Burt looked like, although I knew some of the songs he'd written. "Wives and Lovers"..."Walk On By"..."Don't Make Me Over". When he finally came to California, we met for a drink, then agreed that I would call him if I ever went to New York. Six months later, he came back out here and asked for a dinner date. We went out and had a real good time. He kissed me good-night and the bells went off." The couple married after what Angie described as "a real whirlwind romance."

They were married for 15 years and Angie told me that though she did her best to make it work, a series of difficult circumstances resulted in their eventual divorce.

Since the song, "Raindrops Keep Falling On My Head" is one of my favorites, I enjoyed having Angie tell me about Burt writing it in the lower level room where he kept his piano.

"Although he didn't actually write all the lyrics, he would play those certain notes over and over and they really made you think of raindrops," she said.

Angie has had her share of sadness, coping with the problems of her beloved only daughter Nikki, born three months prematurely, who passed away in 2007, and with a sister suffering with Alzheimer's.

I spent some extra time alone with Angie, helping with information she dictated to me for a possible autobiography. However, when the publisher she was dealing with asked for information she refused to reveal, the project was called off. If such a book resulted in being written, I do not know about it.

Angie's career has included about 50 motion pictures including *Rio Bravo,* with John Wayne, Dean Martin and Ricky Nelson, *Dressed To Kill* with Michael Caine, and *Big Bad Mama,* numerous television roles, and, of course, her portrayal of Sgt. Leann "Pepper" Anderson in the above-mentioned *Police Woman series.*

Chapter 39
The Essence of Eva Gabor

Like most people, I knew Eva Gabor best from watching the *Green Acres* TV series in which she portrayed the sophisticated New Yorker Lisa Douglas, wife of Oliver Wendell Douglas (played by Eddie Albert), who wheedled her into moving to the country.

In real life, she might not have minded that happening so much. She had once grown corn and raised chickens on her two acre Bel Air estate and still had a small vegetable garden there as well as a greenhouse with prize-winning orchids. She had lots of trees, including some bearing fruit, and she was very fond of her good-sized rose garden. On the other hand, when Ralph decided to photograph her among those posies, I was given the responsibility of holding a parasol over her head between shots to protect her from the sun's rays.

Actually both the roses and the parasol were important in her life. One of the deep pink roses in her garden had been named in honor of her by the American Rose Society. The parasol was one from her small, but select collection of more than two dozen of them which she had acquired from all over the world.

Perhaps unfairly, Eva (pronounced as if the E is a long A, in case you aren't aware) was considered notorious for having five husbands (one at a time, of course). I say "unfairly," as many more recently famous actresses and actors, too, have been married nearly as many times and even more so in some cases.

The first time Ralph and I pulled up in front of her large white two story house with Tara-like pillars, which was said to have once belonged to Frank Sinatra, we found ourselves in for some pleasant surprises.

I recalled how beautiful the Hungarian blond actress had been in the 1958 movie musical *Gigi*. Now, in her seventies, she appeared just the same. (Don't ask me how.) She was also good-humored and fun to be with.

Born in Budapest and the youngest of three sisters (Magda and Zsa Zsa were the other two), Eva was the most successful when it came to show business. She had dreamed of becoming an actress from the time she was four. Her career to date at that time included several movies, along with Broadway and TV credits. She'd even done voice-overs for animated films. My favorite of those was *The Aristocats* in which she supplied the voice for the mother cat. Besides speaking "cat," she could converse in English, French, German, and Hungarian.

Eva had an office in a building separate from her house, where we went to take some pictures. She shared her home with four dogs and three cats. She was very active with a number of charitable causes, including the Foundation for Hospice and Homecare. And, in 1984, she had been given a star on the Hollywood Walk of Fame.

The other, most impressive thing about Eva was the wig company of which she had by then been chairman of the board for the past 23 years. She told me how it had come about.

"I was working on *Green Acres* when two very proper gentlemen approached and said they would like me to go into the wig business," she said. "I had done a lot of costume plays on Broadway and the wigs I wore were so heavy, the perspiration used to pour off my face. So I told them, 'If the wigs can weigh an ounce and a half, I will.'

"Where that came from, I don't know. But now they do weigh an ounce and a half and you can't even tell you are wearing a wig. I wear them a lot when I'm traveling."

Eva told me she was working on a novel and I recalled reading her autobiography, named *Orchids and Salami*, which she had written while still in her 20s.

"It was named for the only items that my friends said were always in my refrigerator," she explained, adding that the book was "boring," since it had been written so early in her life.

Referring to her *Green Acres* stint (1965 to 1971) as "a happy six years," Eva said, "There was never a cross word on the set."

Regarding her costume on the show, she explained that the part had originally been written for an American girl, but she was to fashion it into a kooky character all her own.

"They asked me if I had ever been to a farm and I said, 'Yes.' They said, 'What did you wear?' I said, 'Well, I just got up and I went out to see the chickens, still wearing my nightgown.' So that's how it happened. For six years, I was in a nightgown."

Eva was an enthusiastic tennis player and jogger. She worked out two or three times a week, and walked on her treadmill. She talked about taking walks during intervals of living in New York City, where she was warned against strolling through Central Park.

"I used to have a house on Fifth Avenue, and Jackie Kennedy

moved right next door to me. Her Secret Service men parked in front of my townhouse. Every time she went for a walk, I dashed out and walked along behind. I figured they weren't going to let me be killed, and I told the Secret Service people, 'You're following Jackie, but I'm following you'"

Another form of exercise Eva enjoyed was swimming in her pool.

"I usually swim in my big hat and sunglasses and nothing else," she told me with a laugh. "When helicopters fly over, they stop and circle."

Once, when there happened to be a couple of closer observers, her quick wit saved her from excessive embarrassment.

I never saw Magda, but I knew that Eva and Zsa Zsa looked a lot alike, so I could certainly go along with the story that she related.

"I was swimming in my usual outfit, and I had the feeling somebody was peeking," she explained. "I looked up and there were a couple of hired workmen looking down from my wall. They grinned at me and said, 'Hi, Eva.'

"By now, I'd been in the water for an hour and I couldn't stay in any longer. I was turning purple and my fingers were shriveling up from the water. So I said, 'Not Eva – *Zsa Zsa*.' Then I walked out in my total nudity and put on a towel."

Chapter 40
Star Couples

Mary Ann Mobley and Gary Collins

Ralph and I visited this couple at their comfortable Los Angeles area home on assignment for a *Mature American* cover story in 1991.

We already knew that Mary Ann had been the 1959 Miss America , and had an acting career that included Broadway productions such as *Girl Happy* with Elvis Presley, and the TV series *Diff'rent Strokes, Falcon Crest* and *Designing Women*.

One of Gary's movies was *The Longest Day* and his TV series included *The Wackiest Ship in the Army* and *The Iron Horse.* And he was currently hosting ABC's *The Home Show*.

That day we learned that the couple had, by then, been married 24 years and had a 22-year-old daughter named Clancy. In 1962, Mary Ann had been diagnosed with ileitis (inflammation of a portion of the small intestine) and, although she was then in remission, she planned her diet to stay that way. She also spoke to others with similar illnesses. Gary had been the first television host to report on the AIDS epidemic and had received honors for his coverage. And both of them spent a lot of time traveling to give speeches and attend charitable fund raising events.

Gary said that he was very much into running and had participated in several marathons. He also "loved" playing golf.

Another family favorite sport was scuba diving.

"I had a chance to swim with sharks when we visited Epcot Center," remarked Mary Ann. "I've got a tape of me doing it."

When we looked at her askance, she exclaimed, "Sharks are by nature unaggressive creatures, safer to dive with than dolphins, which, in their friendly exuberance, can actually break a diver's ribs."

Other activities pursued by the adventurous brunette were para-sailing and riding cutting horses and Tennessee walking horses.

Ralph took pictures of the two of them working out at their new home gym. And Gary, who claimed he did most of the family cooking, insisted upon giving me a package of raw fish that he recommended I take home and cook.

Mary Ann credited Gary with helping her through the bad times when she had lacked even the energy to get out of bed, and encouraging her to eat more healthful foods.

She made the following comment:

"If you see a turtle sitting on top of a fencepost, you know he didn't get up there by himself."

"I don't know what that means," interjected Gary, "but I love it."

Cyd Charisse and Tony Martin

If I had known that Cyd Charisse's husband, singer Tony Martin, would be at home that day, I probably would have suggested that Ralph and I interview them as a couple for *Mature American magazine*.

As it was, our assignment was for Cyd by herself.

And, although Tony sat beside her in their elegant 3,000 square-foot high-rise condo, he really didn't say much. Located on the 14th floor, their quarters had a view of the Santa Monica Mountains.

Cyd explained that, for most of the years of their marriage back in 1948, they had lived in quite large houses, but that, three years ago, following the death of a prized employee, they had decided that their frequent travels made a different lifestyle more feasible. Cyd's tiny Yorkshire terrier had been on hand to greet us.

"I got her while I was in New York doing *Grand Hotel*," said Cyd. "I named her for my character, Ilizavet, which is Russian. She's a backstage dog. Every time the music started, she knew she wasn't supposed to bark. Now, I take her to exercise class with me and the minute the music starts she runs and jumps in her basket. When the music stops, she's up and ready to go."

About her own name, which was originally Tula Ellice Finklea, she explained, "They always called me 'Sid,' which was the way my older brother said 'sister.' Hollywood later changed the spelling." Her surname Charisse came with her first husband, Nico Charisse, her ballet instructor, whom she married while touring Europe with the Ballet Russe.

Some of her many motion pictures included *Singin' In The Rain, The Band Wagon*, and *Brigadoon*.

"I'm one of the few dancers who had occasion to perform with both Fred Astaire and Gene Kelly," she told us. "In my opinion, they were the two greatest dancers ever to appear on the screen, although they were quite different. Astaire had the better coordination and, while he was very good at choreographing dances for himself and a partner, Kelly's choreographing talent was extended to creating routines for others as well as himself. And Kelly was also the stronger at lifting a partner."

Cyd was a corporate executive for a product she had caused to be created in her effort to relieve her mother's painful arthritis. Named Arctic Spray, it was the result of her urging a regarded chemist to develop the formula to soothe aches and pains. (I tried it and believe it is still available today.)

The couple frequently performed together in nightclubs, and had also collaborated on a book entitled *The Two of Us*, published in 1976.

Steve Allen and Jayne Meadows

I went alone to visit Steve Allen and his wife, Jayne Meadows, and found myself in for a real surprise. As I drove up their hillside drive-way that curved around to the back of their San Fernando Valley home, I looked across their huge backyard and into a neighboring large, tree-and-flower adorned yard, which, for some reason, seemed very familiar.

Mentioning that fact to Steve, I learned the reason.

"For many years, that property belonged to Gale Storm and her husband," he told me."

"Of course," I said. "I visited her there several times many years ago." What had confused me was the fact that I had arrived on their street from the opposite direction. (Widowed and remarried by now, Gale had moved down to a home in Laguna Nigel.)

The year was 1997 and I was writing an article for *Active Times*, a Sunday supplement that appeared in a number of newspapers throughout the country.

Seated together with me, the Allens told me they had by then been married for 40 years.

Their joint professional credits were extremely numerous. Steve, whom Noel Coward had described as "the most talented man in America," was the creator and long-time host of TV's *The Tonight Show*, author of 48 books, composer of 6,000 songs and the scores for several Broadway and TV musicals, playwright, poet, emcee, lecturer, actor, comedian, and lyricist. He also played in big band jazz concerts.

Jayne was a Broadway comedy star in her teens and long-term panelist of *I've Got A Secret*. Her recent movie credits included *De Capo, Murder By Numbers, Casino, The Player*, and the role of Billy Crystal's mother in *City Slickers*. She had just spent six years touring with her one-woman show, *Powerful Women in History*.

Steve was the father of three grown sons from his former marriage to Dorothy Goodman and the couple shared another son, Bill. Together, they had a dozen grandchildren at that time.

"Those who work in creative arts are really lucky," Steve said. "I just do the things I love to do and it works out nicely. The world pays me for them."

"Steve is easy to live with," offered Jayne fondly. "Our talents are so different. He is ad-lib and creative. I am a disciplined, dedicated, dramatic character actress who creates roles and was trained to learn lines. So we aren't competing."

Chapter 41
Marion and Mona

Marion Ross

Marion's eleven years of playing Marion Cunningham on the *Happy Days* TV series brought her worldwide recognition, lifetime friends, and a lot of fun. She commemorated it with a special room in her home for various forms of the show's memorabilia.

When Ralph and I wanted to do a cover story on her for *Mature American*, I had only to approach a friend and fellow member of Hollywood Women's Press Club named Barbara Best, who was Marion's personal manager.

One thing led to another and we ended by paying her more than one visit and doing several different stories about her.

One of the most interesting things about the perky red-haired actress was her home, largely because she had helped to design it herself.

Since she already owned one San Fernando Valley house, she had originally purchased this one as a small "investment" rental cottage.

When she decided to turn it into the sort of dream house she'd enjoy living in, she spent lots of time looking around for ideas. She said she'd visit multimillion dollar homes being built in Beverly Hills and ask the contractor to let her take a look.

"As soon as he left the room, I would take off my shoes and sit in the bathtub, or pull out my tape measure and check the size of things. When I found something I liked, I'd call my architect to come and take a look," she told us.

After being combined with a former small garage, the house had been turned into an exceptionally light and airy 4,000 square foot rustic chalet type with spacious rooms, beamed ceilings, sturdy wood posts, a wicker chair-swing, and a graceful stairway, complete with a balcony, leading to her personal second-story quarters. That area included a large combination bedroom-office-sitting room, an elegant bathroom, an outdoor sundeck and a fireplace. Guest bedrooms were in the lower part of the house.

Special features in her large back yard included a park-type yard swing for four, tennis court, flagstone-bordered swimming pool with spa, water fall and a small stone sea otter, fruit trees and flowers. It was a place where she enjoyed entertaining her former *Happy Days* "family" and other friends.

Born in Albert Lea, Minnesota, Marion told us that she had wanted to be an actress since her early childhood. In fact, at the age of 13, she changed the spelling of her name from Marian to Marion because she thought it would look nice on a theater marquee.

After moving to San Diego, California with her family, she became a drama major at San Diego State University and appeared in local theatrical performances. Signed by Paramount Pictures, she had roles in movies that included *Forever Female, Teacher's Pet, Legend of the Incas, Sabrina, The Glenn Miller Story* and *Operation Petticoat*. For television, she portrayed an Irish maid in *Life* with *Father* – the first live series to be aired in color. Following *Happy Days*, she played the bride of Captain Stubing on *The Love Boat* series. She was accepting more movie and TV roles as well as numerous live theater ones.

A divorced "single mother," Marion had raised a son and daughter by herself, but was currently blessed with the companionship of actor Paul Michael, who is said to still be with her at this writing.

Mona Freeman

Since Ralph and I continued to do collector articles for a variety of publications, we visited Mona Freeman's Los Angeles area home to discuss and photograph her collections of Shirley Temple dolls and Raggedy Ann (and Andy) Dolls.

Mona herself had been a young teenage model and then star of several movies for Paramount during the 1940s and '50s. But she said, "As a child, I loved Shirley Temple movies. My favorite toy was my Shirley Temple doll. I still think she was the cutest child star that ever lived. "

Born in Baltimore, Maryland, she had moved with her parents to Pelham, New York, where she caught the eye of John Powers who hired her as a Powers Junior Miss model. Howard Hughes saw her on a magazine cover and signed her to a contract. After he called her to Hollywood, she persuaded him to sell her contract to Paramount Pictures.

Some of the movies she appeared in were *Junior Miss, Mother Wore Tights, Battle Cry, Jumping Jacks,* and *Copper Canyon.*

Married twice, she had a grown-up daughter and four granddaughters by the time we met her. But the names of some of the men she had dated between her divorce and her marriage to her second husband, businessman Jack Ellis, read like a cast of romantic suitors. It included Nicky Hilton, Vic Damone, Frank Sinatra, Bing Crosby and Robert Wagner.

Although Mona declined to watch her own movies on television, she had never lost interest in watching the ones starring Shirley Temple.

She said during a visit to an antique store she considered replacing her long lost doll, but, at first, the prices turned her off.

"My parents had paid just $8 for my first doll and now that store wanted $150. I decided to think it over, but by the time I'd made up my mind to buy one, I had to pay nearly twice that amount.

At the time of our visit, she had nearly 20 of the kind she wanted. They were original dolls of the 1930s, all made by Ideal, ranging in size from 11 inches to 27 inches and, even at that time which was several years ago, they had cost her much more than her initial purchase.

The Raggedy Ann and Andy dolls were largely of the homemade kind. She said that she found them at doll shows, antique shops, yard sales and even in other people's trash.

At least one of our articles dealt with Mona's second career of painting portraits and landscapes. Always interested in art and drawing people, she was specializing in painting children and was busy accepting commissions to do so.

"I take all of my own photographs to paint from and sometimes it takes a lot of time to capture just what I am looking for," she said.

Her clients appreciated her special talent for capturing the inner essence of her subjects as well as their outer appearance.

Chapter 42

Three was Enough for Dick and Pat Van Patten

Dick Van Patten did a great job of portraying the father of eight children in his hit TV series *Eight Is Enough*, but, in real life, he and his wife, Pat were content to call it quits with three sons – Vincent, Nels, and James.

One year Ralph and I did six major articles about Dick Van Patten and it seemed that we were always going to Dick's house. Fortunately, Dick and Pat were good natured about opening the door of their Sherman Oaks area house to find us outside.

But then, they were used to people showing up at their house. Their professional size backyard tennis court was responsible for several of Dick's tennis playing friends coming over frequently to join him in a game. They included Alan Alda, Gene Wilder, Carl Reiner, Mel Brooks, Mariette Hartley and Bernie Koppel (the doctor on *The Love Boat* TV series).

Dick's tennis court was also the setting for some of Ralph's best pictures of Dick and the background for an acrylic painting I did of him (which I hope he still exhibits in his backyard den).

In one of my articles, I likened Dick to the TV battery ad bunny who kept going and going and going. It seemed to me that he hated to sit still when he could be busy or en route to some other place.

"Dickie has to be out there doing something just about all the time, and he's very curious. He doesn't want to miss anything," agreed Pat fondly.

It seemed he had plenty of things to do and places to go to keep him busy.

There was his daily tennis game, a dip in his unheated swimming pool, movie and television roles to play, races to attend to watch his own racehorse, Waterzip, and, lately, meetings regarding the pet food company he had co-founded. (Today, it is not only formulated for dogs and cats, but for tigers and other zoo animals as well.)

Regarding his tennis games, which were one of his favorite activities, his son, James created a humorous video on the subject, called *Dirty Tennis*, co-starring Bruce Jenner.

"Jimmy noticed that I always seem to win and yet the guys I play seem to be much better players," explained Dick. "He realized that I always have the radio playing loud and the phone on the court is always ringing, and I slice the ball and everything."

Other admitted player distractions included Dick's unusual tennis "uniform" – black socks and a bathing suit -- his strategy of arranging that the sun be in his opponent's eyes, and Pat's interrupting the game with the offer of a pitcher of lemonade.

But, humor aside, although Dick might seem like a mild-mannered Clark Kent, he was, in reality, more like that character's alterego, Superman. Raised in New York by a mother who was a physical training teacher and a father who spent every weekend playing tennis, he learned early "how good physical exercise is for you.

"On the coldest day in winter, Dad made me shovel the snow off the handball court so we could play," Dick said.

After vigorous exercise, it was common practice for the Van Pattens to jump into ice cold water. Dick prided himself on being a member of The Penguin Club, which swims in ocean waters all year round, making their annual initial swim on New Year's Day regardless of the weather. And he also ran in frequent 10k races.

Beginning his acting career at the age of seven, Dick was really known as Dickie Van Patten. He appeared in a long line of Broadway shows including *On Borrowed Time, On the Skin of Our Teeth,* and *Mister Roberts.*

He first met Pat – the daughter of a former North Carolina dance school owner, who, along with her brother, was billed as the world's youngest exhibition ballroom dance team – in the eighth grade at a New York professional children's school.

"I didn't really know him," she admitted. "I sat next to him and he used to look at my paper and say, 'What have you got there?' He was never out of a Broadway play, doing the work of an adult, performing every night and matinees, so he didn't have time to do homework.

"Then, later, when I was a June Taylor dancer on *The Jackie Gleason Show* and he was on *I Remember Mama*, our rehearsals overlapped. One day, at the big hall above Grand Central Station, I walk in and he sees me and points to me (he didn't remember me from school), and says to the producer, 'I would marry that girl tomorrow.'

"To me, he said, 'Hi, I'm Dick Van Patten.'

"I said, 'Hi, I'm Pat Poole. We were in the eighth grade together.'

"And he said, 'Oh. Are you married?'

"I said, 'No, I'm engaged. Are you married?'

"He said, 'No.'

"He didn't know what to say next and he was being cagey, so he had the producer of his show call the Jackie Gleason office and find out my phone number and have them call me and ask if I'd like to do the choreography for the *Mama* show that week. (They were doing the Turkey Trot.) So then I go in and rehearse them.

"Then Dick said, 'Aren't you going to come Friday night and see your choreography?'

"So I said, 'Oh yes.' So I go down and take my fiancé. I had no idea what he was trying to do. From there on," she said, "it got complicated."

But their marriage was inevitable.

At the time of our many articles, Dick's career included over 600 radio shows, 27 Broadway plays, nearly 20 feature films, and more than half a dozen television series, as well as numerous guest appearances. His movies included *Spaceballs, Snowball Express, High Anxiety, Soylent Green, Superdad,* and *West World.* He had recently received his own star on the Hollywood Walk of Fame, and he was a spokesperson for Mothers Against Drunk Driving (MAD).

Pat's career included dancing on Broadway in *Me and Juliet,* along with Shirley MacLaine and a role in the Kevin Costner movie, *Bodyguard.* She was one of Farrah Fawcett's best friends.

Ralph and I had the privilege of showing parts of their comfortable home in an article about them for *Valley Magazine.* And we also collaborated on another, featuring Dick and all three of his sons for *Men's Health.*

Chapter 43
Two Ladies from England

Emma Samms

The day that Ralph and I spent with Emma Samms was one of the times when I regretted his friendly schmoozing. By the time he completed his picture taking and talking, I had a mere fifteen minutes left for my formal sit-down interview with Emma. Fortunately, I had been able to garner pertinent information through casual conversation with her and her representative, along with printed hand-out biographies.

By this time in our joint careers, Ralph and I were accustomed to the stars that we interviewed telling us that we knew more other stars than they did. It did seem that this was generally true as we went from one to another while most of them only had occasion to become acquainted with the ones they worked with or were able to meet socially. Name dropping and comparing notes regarding those they also knew or didn't know had become part of the game.

As usual, we produced more than one article about Emma with various slants including the home she had chosen for herself and a major charitable organization she had co-founded with her cousin Peter Samuelson.

Emma's birth name was Emma Samuelson, but it became necessary for her to change it when she registered with the American actor's union Equity as they already had someone with her real name.

Born into a British theatrical family, with a mother who had been a featured soloist with the Royal Ballet Company, Emma began ballet lessons at the age of two and was accepted by the Royal Ballet School when she was eleven, but after six more years of training, she suffered a serious hip injury that forced her to give up the dream of becoming a prima ballerina and choreographer.

She then took pre-med classes in England and, at the time of our interview was a certified emergency medical technician who volunteered her services whenever possible.

Emma went into modeling and had appeared in many fashion magazines. Then she went on to acting. After coming to America, she had appeared on *General Hospital, Hotel,* the *Ellis Island* miniseries, and had a starring role, portraying Fallon Carrington Colby on the ABC-TV series *Dynasty II: The Colbys.*

The 6,500 square foot home she had purchased was perched on the edge of a canyon in mountains overlooking the San Fernando Valley. She was having fun furnishing it and had also recently taken up ice skating. And she had adopted two large mixed breed dogs from Lifelines For Pets.

It was back at the opening of her first film, *Arabian Adventure,* in England, an event that was a benefit for a children's hospital that brought about her decision to found the organization called Starlight.

"I went to the hospital for a visit and it was there that I met a desperately ill 12-year-old boy named Sean. He became my friend and I visited him often," she told me.

Emma continued to write to Sean after moving to the United States and was saddened to learn that his condition had worsened. With the help of her cousin Peter, she arranged for Sean and his mother to be flown to this country so he could enjoy the fun of going to Disneyland. His 10-day trip even included a helicopter ride. Unfortunately, Sean had little time left.

"The Starlight Foundation name is derived from that old childhood poem "Starlight, star-bright, first star I see tonight, I wish I may, I wish I might have the wish I wish tonight," said Emma.

Today, Starlight Children's Foundation has chapters and offices throughout the United States, Canada, the United Kingdom, Australia, and Japan with the aim of providing education, entertainment, and family events to help children cope with the pain, fear, and isolation of prolonged illness.

Lynn Redgrave

Lynn and her then husband, actor/director John Clark, were living in a sprawling split-level hillside house on five acres, situated in the Santa Monica Mountains in the outskirts of Los Angeles, when Ralph and I visited them.

"On a clear day, you can see Catalina Island through a break in the foothills," Lynn told us.

Also occupying the country-like five bedroom house were their three children – Benjamin, 24, Kelly, 22, and Annabel, 11. The couple had been married 26 years at the time of our visit.

Outbuildings included a large office for John and quarters for the family riding horses, dogs, rabbits, ducks and chickens. On a lower level were the swimming pool, sauna and tennis courts.

Since I have always loved to ride horses, but never had occasion to own one, I truly envied Lynn when she told us about riding her sorrel mare, Minerva, on nearby state park trails.

Lynn showed us through the house, which contained many unusual "treasures," including an old wood-burning stove, which they found in Kentucky and an attractive stained-glass light fixture that Lynn said they had discovered in a dump.

At that time, Lynn and John were planning a six-week, 30-cities tour with her show, *Shakespeare for my Father*, directed by John.

"I think of it as a living memorial to my father, Sir Michael Redgrave, who was considered one of England's great actors. He was knighted by Queen Elizabeth for his services to the theatre," she explained.

Lynn was also anticipating being seen in a three-part mini-series thriller entitled *Calling The Shots*, to air on *Masterpiece Theatre*. Her early movies had included *Tom Jones* and *Georgy Girl*.

Her role in the American TV series *House Calls* brought her to the attention of American audiences, but ended by producing a major problem for her. Lynn was fired when she insisted upon breast-feeding her then baby, Annabel, during breaks on the set.

Later, Lynn became well known for a series of commercials for Heinz Foods, manufacturer of weight loss foods for Weight Watchers. Her signature line was "This is living" and she used it for the title of a book she wrote about her life experiences, which was published in 1991.

Lynn is a naturalized American citizen. In 2000, she was named an Officer of the Order of the British Empire by Queen Elizabeth II. She and John were divorced in 2000. Before her death in 2010, Redgrave had appeared in the TV series *Desperate Housewives* and *Ugly Betty*

Chapter 44

Moore and Mayo

Both of these beautiful blond actresses were senior citizens by the time I got around to interviewing them and, though each was dynamic in her own way, they were strikingly different personality-wise. My interviews of each were totally separate from each other.

Terry Moore

Prior to meeting Terry, I had known her mostly as the heroine of one of my favorite movies – *Mighty Joe Young,* a more lovable and quite a bit smaller version of the scary King Kong of my youth. Actually, by the time I met her she had already appeared in around 70 movies and a television series called *Empire.*

She had recently co-starred in a movie called *Beverly Hills Brats*, along with Martin Sheen and Peter Billingsley, which she had produced with Jerry Rivers.

Ralph and I got together with her more than once and produced a variety of articles about her. We saw Jerry Rivers, who was 20 years younger than Terry, nearly every time we saw her. According to how you looked at it, he became either her fifth or sixth husband. Terry had lived with the world-famous Howard Hughes for a time at his Tule Springs Ranch near Las Vegas, Nevada. After his death, in 1976, she claimed the pair had been secretly married and never divorced. Although she failed to produce any proof of that fact, his estate paid her a settlement in 1984, the same year as her book about him, *The Beauty and the Billionaire,* came out.

Not only that, she had claimed that Hughes had been denied necessary medical treatment by the people surrounding him. And she considered him her true soul-mate who was watching over her beyond the grave. She was even to write a second book entitled *The Passions of Howard Hughes.*

Terry was very involved with looking into what she believed to be her past lives and had undergone hypnosis with Jess Stearn (a prolific writer who had developed an interest in psychic phenomena and reincarnation) to do so.

Regarding Hughes, Terry told me, "Howard was my karmic soul-mate, somebody I had to learn with. He said he felt he'd always known me and that there was a great karmic tie between us. "

As advised by Stearn, she considered Jerry Rivers "a companion soul-mate; a positive force with none of the resentment of karmic soul-mates."

Terry was born Helen Koford in Glendale, California, was a child model and began acting in movies at the age of eleven. Her grownup leading men included Burt Lancaster, Robert Wagner, Tyrone Power, Fred Astaire and Glenn Ford. Other of her movies were *Beneath the Twelve Mile Reef, Daddy Long Legs,* and *Come Back, Little Sheba,* for which she was nominated for an Academy Award.

The mother of two sons, Terry had appeared on the cover of *Playboy* magazine at the age of 55 as a way of defying the show business belief that actresses were "washed up" at a much earlier age than their male counterparts.

Virginia Mayo

Ralph and I drove to Thousand Oaks, a town west of the San Fernando Valley, to visit Virginia Mayo in the home she was then sharing with her daughter, Mary, her son-in-law, and her three young grandsons.

Unlike so many of the actresses we had met, Virginia had had only one husband – the love of her life, actor Michael O'Shea. The couple had met early in her career, on the set of the 1943 movie *Jack London*. He had the title role and she played his first love. They started dating in real life and were married in 1947.

Born Virginia Clara Jones in St. Louis, Missouri, she began acting and tap dancing at the age of six at her aunt's School of Dramatic Expression. Later, she toured the United States as a dancer, changing her last name to match that of other act members. She was performing in Billy Rose's revue at his Diamond Horseshoe nitery when Samuel Goldwyn offered her a Hollywood contract.

Seated on a couch in her living room, we discussed her life with her husband and her movie career.

"I was never really a Hollywood person," she explained. "I loved making movies and it was fun shooting on location but I didn't go to parties much." (I could certainly sympathize as I have never been a party person myself.)

Virginia had played leading lady to such comedians as Bob Hope and Danny Kaye in color extravaganzas of the 1940s. Some of her movies were *The Secret Life of Walter Mitty* and *The Princess and the Pirate.* More recently at that time were occasional appearances in such episodic television shows as *Murder, She Wrote.*

"I was disappointed when my movie career ended in the 1960s when television threw the studios into a panic and they began cancelling contracts," she said. "My husband passed away in 1973. I still get some television and stage roles, and, in my spare time, I read and do some oil painting."

She told me that she had received a lot of fan mail over the years.

"My favorite was one from the Sultan of Morocco. He said my beauty was tangible proof of the existence of God."

She sighed. "I should have kept that letter, but I never liked clutter, and I threw out almost everything that pertained to my career, including all my old scripts."

Nicholas Savalas, Shirley, and Tori Spelling

Eva Gabor with Shirley

Shirley with Angie Dickinson

Marion Ross with Shirley

Betty White with Shirley

Shirley with Anne Francis

Donald O'Connor with Shirley

Dolores and Bob Hope with pet dogs

Robert Stack with Shirley

Shirley with Rod Taylor

Nanette Fabray with Shirley

Gail and David Carridine on their ranch

Janet Leigh with Shirley

Orson Bean with Shirley

John Forsythe with Shirley

The hubcap Pegasus on the ranch of Jack Palance

Lynn Redgrave at home in her canyon

Shirley with Fess Parker at his winery

Shirley with Earl Holliman

Shirley with Joan and George Kennedy

Chapter 45

Fabray and Fabares

I had the pleasure of writing about two related actresses -- Nanette Fabray and her niece Shelley Fabares. Both share the same last name, except for the spelling. And both started out with the same spelling (and pronunciation) but Nanette decided to change hers. Read further for an explanation as to why.

Nanette Fabray

On assignment for what turned out to be the spring 1995 issue cover story of *Mature American* magazine, Ralph and I paid a visit to the Pacific Palisades home of Nanette Fabray.

As we stood in her tree and flower filled half-acre yard, she indicated an impressive mansion on the other side of the wall.

"That 6,000-square-foot house was my home for several years," she said. "After my husband, Randy (screen writer Ranald MacDougall) died in 1973, I sold that house and built this one on part of the property. When we lived there, we filled every bit of space with Randy's mother, my father, my three stepchildren, and our son, Jamie. Since I now live alone, this 3,000-square-foot place is large enough. "

The Broadway, motion picture, and television actress told us the story of her name-spelling change.

She had been touring the country in a show called *Meet The People*, which later opened in New York.

"I agreed to perform for a benefit at Madison Square Garden at which Eleanor Roosevelt was the keynote speaker," she related. "When it came time for my introduction by Ed Sullivan (famous for his mispronunciation of names) I was waiting in the wings to go on.

"He had my card in his hand and he said, 'Ladies and gentlemen, let's welcome this nice young lady, opening this week in a new show – Miss Nanette' He looked down at the card and spelled 'F-A-B-A-R-E-S – Miss Nanette Fa Bare Ass.'"

Not having heard his introduction, Nanette came onstage and began to sing an operatic selection. To her horror, she heard catcalls from the rear of the audience, apparently from somebody who mistook her for an opera-singing stripper. "Come on, Baby, let's see what you can do." As the jeering continued, she burst into tears and ran from the stage, right into the arms of the watching Mrs. Roosevelt.

"Why do you cry?" she was asked. "You *must* do something about your name."

"The next day, I changed it to F-A-B-R-A-Y."

Nanette went on to star in 11 Broadway Shows. She made several movies, including *Harper Valley PTA* and *Cockeyed Cowboys of Calico County*, with Dan Blocker. The latter was written and directed by her husband. For television, she portrayed Bonnie Franklin's mother, Katherine Romano, on *One Day at a Time*.

Nanette was still in her early 20s, and already a sought-after Broadway actress, when she discovered she had a serious hearing problem.

"In those days, you had to present a perfect image, so I kept it a secret as long as I could," she recalled. "On stage, I was all right, because people would speak up. But I finally had to start wearing hearing-aids for the rest of the time. I was the first celebrity to admit that I had something wrong with me, and the press attacked me for that. But I thought it was important to show that you could be young and successful and still have what was then called an impairment or a handicap."

At one time, she was the chairman of The National Council on Deaf Education and she was also one of the founding members of the National Captioning Institute, which is responsible for the public law stating that, starting in 1994, all TV sets must be equipped for captioning.

At the time of our interview, she had endured four operations and had excellent hearing, but she was, nevertheless, becoming a spokesperson for people dealing with disabilities.

Shelley Fabares

I had conducted a telephone interview with Shelley Fabares for a *Woman's World* story in 1994. It was ten years after her marriage to the handsome actor/director/producer Mike Farrell and during her portrayal of Christine Armstrong on the ABC television series *Coach.*

To my knowledge, Shelley had not experienced a similar difficulty with her birth name. However, she had been dealing with other problems that she related to me. A professional actress since the age of three, she already had appeared in half a dozen TV series, including *The Donna Reed Show.*

"About the time of my marriage to Mike, my 'other mother,'

Donna Reed, died of breast cancer," she began. "My real mother appeared to be descending into madness and was finally discovered to have Alzheimer's disease. In 1988, at about the same time I got my latest series, I was going from the extreme of having two stepchildren who didn't want me around to having wonderfully loving relationships with me. And, in 1992, my mother died."

Some of those events were responsible for Shelley becoming seriously involved with charitable associations.

"I work all year round on the board of directors of the National Alzheimer's Association, traveling about to help raise awareness of the public to what Alzheimer's is and what it isn't. I also try to inform family members of Alzheimer's victims about what the Association can do to help them in their roles of caretakers," she said. "In addition, I am involved with the Donna Reed Association For Cancer."

Shelley told me about a serious accident she had recently suffered.

It seemed that, while inspecting the remodeling of a second floor bathroom with her architect, she missed her footing and fell between two of the joists in an area where the floorboards had been removed.

"I crashed through the ceiling of the first floor and would have crashed through the first floor into the basement if the architect hadn't grabbed my wrist. I broke the ribs on my left side, threw my back out, and damaged my liver and spleen and other soft tissue in the area. I was in bed for about two months of my summer hiatus and got back on my feet just in time for the show's new season."

On the bright side, she was enthusiastic about both her loving husband and her TV role on *Coach*.

Chapter 46

The Flexible Fess Parker

"Come on up."

The slightly crooked genial smile of the six-foot, six-inch-tall silver-haired gentleman looking down from the balcony above his gracious two-story high tasting room was appealingly familiar.

The year was 1996 and Ralph and I had journeyed for miles through the rolling hills of the world-renowned Santa Ynez Valley – home to such notables as Michael Jackson, John and Bo Derek and John Forsythe – to reach the Fess Parker Winery and Vineyard. We'd found his ranch with its ancient live oak trees, manicured lawns, and flowerbeds enhancing the huge English colonial style building sporting wide, shady verandas, both impressive and inviting.

We climbed the stairway and followed Fess into his cozy office. There were comfortable couches for guests, but, behind the desk, stood a 100-year-old throne-like chair that had been chosen to accommodate his lengthy frame.

Photos on the walls gave evidence of his earlier career. They showed Fess dressed as Davy Crockett for movies and television of the 1950s and as Daniel Boone for the series of that name which began in 1964 and ran for six years.

Fess told us that he began buying real estate in 1953 and working in commercial real estate in 1961. He had moved to Santa Barbara in 1958 but went back to Los Angeles during the first three years of *Daniel Boone*. But, later, with two young children, he decided that Santa Barbara was a better family location.

Born in Texas, Fess was named for his father and told us that his first name was an old English surname meaning "proud."

"I liked it so much that I named my son Fess Elisha Parker III, but we call him Eli," he said.

He enlisted in the U.S. Navy in 1943, which gave him the opportunity to visit the Hollywood Canteen and a couple of studios. "That's when I kind of got interested in show business," he remarked..

"I was studying at an aviation radio gunner's school in Tennessee when somebody looked at me and said 'You know, you don't fit in the airplane too well.'" For three years, he was shifted about the country doing general detail before being sent overseas, and said he was in the middle of the Pacific when they dropped the bomb that ultimately ended World War II.

Later, after graduating from the University of Texas, he worked on a master's degree at the University of Southern California. He began his acting career as a stage performer in the national company of *Mister Roberts*, and his film debut in *Untamed Frontier*. Spotted by Disney while doing a small part in a film named *Them*, he was signed to play the title role in *Davy Crockett. King of the Wild Frontier*. Other movies included *Battle Cry, The Kid From Left Field, The Great Locomotive Chase, Westward Ho! The Wagons*, and *The Light in the Forest*.

Fess said that he had been put into many situations that he had not anticipated, especially when he and his "sidekick," portrayed by Buddy Ebsen, were sent out on the road to premiere the Davy Crockett picture.

"They said, 'You recorded "The Ballad of Davy Crockett." Do your little song. You and Buddy make up a little act and go out and do it.'"

After doing their show for two nights at the Hollywood Bowl (performing for crowds of 25,000 people each night), they toured 13 foreign countries and 42 cities, including Tokyo, Japan.

By the time of our interview, Fess was moving into the field of real estate in a big way, having completed developments that included three large mobile home parks and the 360 room Fess Parker's Red Lion Resort across the street from the beach in Santa Barbara.

"In the early 1970s, I had reached a point where I thought it was not likely I would receive the kind of opportunities that would keep me interested in acting," he said.

Fess admitted that he chose to go into the winery business "at an age when most people might be thinking, 'How can I get rid of responsibility and take it easy?'

"It was an opportunity to go into business with my son, who was 26 when we started.

"I was raised on a farm, and I'd bought the ranch because I wanted to live out here. In the beginning, there was just the two of us. We hired the wine maker to put n the vineyards and oversee the construction of the buildings. Now, my son is the wine maker. Our wines have won 10 gold medals, 15 silvers, and 14 bronzes all over the United States. Our Pinot Noir, Chardonnay, and Syrah are particularly popular with the critics." In addition, at that time, the winery was also producing Johannesberg Riesling, Merlot, and Muscat Canelli.

Fess told us that unusual climatic conditions served to make his area notably exceptional for raising certain varieties.

"It has to do with Santa Barbara's south-facing coast and the mountain range which is unusual in that it runs due east and west. When you round Point Conception, where the coast line switches to north and south, we have a colder, deeper, bluer Pacific, but we still have the southern California climate. We have the marine influence, but a longer growing period than other areas."

Both father and son had their homes on the ranch, and Fess said he visited his Santa Barbara hotel about once a week. The winery was a favorite place for visitors from all over the world to visit and tour as well as mingle with their famous host.

Before leaving, Ralph and I were taken on a tour of the entire establishment by Fess, who presented us with bottles of wine, which, as I recall, was some of the best I have ever tasted.

Later, I read that the former 714 acreage of the property had been increased to 1,500 acres, and that Fess owned the Fess Parker's Wine Country Inn and Spa.

Sadly, while completing the writing of this book in 2010, the world learned that Fess Parker had passed away.

Chapter 47

Remarkable Robert Stack

Handsome actor Robert Stack turned out to be one of the peo-
ple I wrote a number of articles about. Ralph and I visited his Bel
Air home in 1996 and our first article was a cover story for *Mature
American* magazine. Several more followed, but my final article on
him was a sad experience, since it was a tribute to that patriotic
American written for *Airport Journals*, following his death in 2003,

When Ralph and I arrived at the Stack home, we were met at
the door by the actor himself and his tiny miniature Yorkshire Terrier named Bravo Gianni. We quickly learned the story behind that
name. While visiting in the south of France with his owner, the
little dog had successfully negotiated a precarious rail-less circu-
lar staircase, causing witnesses to exclaim "Bravo, Gianni."

"I've been married to Rosemarie for 40 years and we've lived in
this house most of that time," Bob remarked. "The original house
and property belonged to the early film star Colleen Moore. We
sold off part of it and had this house constructed in between the
tennis court and the pool."

A confirmed bachelor until well into his 30s, Bob admitted
to, at one time, ridiculing his friends who were preoccupied with

their wives. In retaliation, he was told that one day he would find the right girl and learn what it was like.

He did…and he did. Introduced to the beautiful blond actress Rosemarie Bowe by his agent, he fell in love for real and finally told her, "I have to marry you." He then proceeded to go overboard in doing the family bit, diapering and doting on both their two children, Elizabeth and Charles Robert.

"I was *more* married than all the guys I knew," he said with a laugh.

Bob told us that he enjoyed being host of the *Unsolved Mysteries* TV series because it meant playing a part in apprehending criminals.

"The show has been responsible for catching over 41 percent of the fugitives profiled on the series since its premiere," he said.

"Police and the FBI are standing by when our show is on the air to be available for call-ins from the viewing public, who are invited to offer information. The viewers are the ones who make it happen," he said.

Bob told us that he was a fifth generation Californian on his mother's side. In fact, the first frame house to be built in the city of Los Angeles (which has been relocated into the historic Heritage Square) had belonged to his family. Bob's father, James Langford Stack, was a successful self-made Irish businessman and a close friend to Will Rogers, George Bancroft, Mack Sennett and Leo Carrillo.

Only three-years-old when his parents divorced, Bob was taken to Europe for four years by his mother, while his older brother, James Jr. stayed with his father. As a young child, he learned to speak French and Italian but did not learn English until he returned to the United States.

He chuckled as he recalled, "Mother had no passport for me

and by now I was seven and too old to travel on hers. I was held at Ellis Island and dear Mama was accused of trying to bring in an illegal émigré. I howled in all the wrong languages until I was finally rescued by my grandfather."

Although his parents remarried, Bob's father died when he was only nine. So that her sons would enjoy the benefits of male influence, his mother encouraged them to take part in various athletics. He became a National Skeet Shooting Champion and holder of two world records at the age of 16. He also became a leading speedboat racer on the West Coast. And, on entering the University of Southern California, became one of the stars of the polo team.

While taking voice lessons, at the request of his mother, Bob had occasion to visit Universal Studios where he was approached by Producer Joe Pasternak, who offered him a screen test. This resulted in him giving Deanna Durbin (America's Sweetheart at that time) her first movie kiss in the 1939 picture *First Love*

Bob told us a few more of his fond memories regarding other famous "household names." He taught Carole Lombard to shoot when he was only 13, became chums with Judy Garland, dated Betty Grable, knew Marilyn Monroe when she was still Norma Jean Dougherty, and protected an underage Gloria De Haven from the advances of Errol Flynn. He played polo with Spencer Tracy, hunted ducks with Clark Gable and shared his bachelor quarters on occasion with the young Jack Kennedy. He and his mother befriended the actress Nancy Davis on her arrival in Hollywood and Bob says he was so impressed with Ronald Reagan's negotiating skills while he headed the Screen Actors' Guild that he advised him to go into politics.

Bob's long list of movie roles includes one in *The High and the Mighty*, a favorite of mine. And his portrayal of Eliot Ness in the television series *The Untouchables* earned him the praise of doing "a fine job" from that gentleman's widow.

One of the reasons I was to write my tribute to Robert Stack as a patriotic American was his four year stint in the U.S. Navy during World War II. Later, as a civilian, he toured Vietnam, visiting and giving moral support to a large number of wounded young men.

For people wishing to read more about Bob Stack's interesting life, I recommend his autobiography *Straight Shooting*.

Chapter 48

Stars Fond of Fitness

I interviewed and wrote about many fitness fanciers but the following are some of the most prominent.

Jack LaLanne

Ralph and I met with "the godfather of fitness," as he was sometimes called, and his wife Elaine, in the lobby of the Sportsman's Lodge Hotel in the San Fernando Valley. They had occasion to be visiting our area, down from their Morro Bay home.

A doctor of chiropractic and a fitness, exercise, and nutritional expert, who had hosted his own TV show from 1951 to 1985, Jack was then in his 80s. He was famous for his many feats of strength and fitness over 30 years, generally performed on or near a birthday. Here are just two examples.

At the age of 40, he swam the entire length of the Golden Gate Bridge underwater, with 140 pounds of equipment -- a world record. At age 70, handcuffed and shackled, fighting strong winds and currents, he swam 1.5 miles while towing 70 boats with 70 people from Queensway Bay Bridge in Long Beach Harbor to the Queen Mary ship.

Richard Simmons

In 1986, the year that Ralph and I visited the Tara-like white pillared home of Richard Simmons, he was concentrating on what he termed "the year for the physically challenged."

His goal was to make their lives "a little better" by creating a fitness exercise program for people with a wide range of disabilities, and also to "make them laugh."

He told us that profits from his most recent book, *Reach for Fitness*, would be donated to the funding of exercise classes and programs for the physically challenged, to be offered through a system of hospitals and YMCAs across the country.

And, as often was the case, one of our goals was to talk with him about his collections.

Richard confessed that he had fallen in love with Dalmatian dogs after seeing the Disney movie, *101 Dalmatians*. He not only had five of those real live dogs, he had a number of toy Dalmatians scattered throughout his light and airy home, as well as a collection of china ones. Other collections included 2,000 original photos of Barbra Streisand (whom he particularly admired), and an accumulation of pig figurines.

Since Richard had suffered from overweight as a teenager, he said, "I collect pigs because I used to be a little oink-oink before I lost all that weight and became interested in proper diet and healthful exercise."

Martin Kove

Our interview with Martin Kove resulted in the February, 1990 cover story of *Mature Health* magazine on which he was pictured jogging.

Because the three original *Karate Kid* movies are still often seen on television, you might know him best for playing John Kreese, the vicious karate instructor who immortalized the command "No mercy."

In real life, Marty, as we came to know him, turned out to be an all-round nice fellow. He was a proud stepfather to Sean, the teenage son of his wife Vivienne, and father to their twin babies, Jesse and Rachael, born that year.

The actor told us that he had wanted to make the above-mentioned character in the *Karate Kid* movies a little bit more likable.

"But every time I tried to," he explained, "the director would stop me and say, 'Marty, I want him pure.' The purity of his evil was considered to be something that made him very interesting to audiences," he added.

Marty did have other opportunities to make nice, however. He portrayed a fun-loving cop on the *Cagney and Lacey* TV series for six years and an innocent alien on his own series, *Hard Time on Planet Earth*.

A holder of honorary black belts in Okinawa-te and Tiger-kempo karate, he said he preferred the challenge of Kendo – Japanese sword fighting -- for which he attended classes.

Since our article was for a health publication, we discussed his healthy diet and five-times-a-week 30 minute non-stop workout of lifting weights, running in place, and doing crunches, sit-ups, presses and curls.

Suzanne Somers

You may recall that this co-star of the *Three's Company* TV series had first come to public attention when playing the mysterious blond driving a

Thunderbird in George Lucas' movie *American Graffiti* back in 1973.

I wrote more than one published article on Suzanne Somers, although I never actually met her in person.

Our first conversation was a standard telephone one, but, later, when I needed to update, we shared what I consider one of my most unusual interviews.

Since she was in the process of packing to leave on her annual two month European vacation, she agreed to talk with me from a phone in her car while completing some last minute errands. (She didn't say who was driving her around.)

"If I lose you, I'll call you right back," she promised.

In 1986, Suzanne had written an autobiographical book, *Keeping Secrets,* dealing with how her father's alcoholism affected her growing- up years, with the happy ending of his eventual "cure." It was published in 1988 and made into a television movie which she produced and starred in.

In 1996, another book of hers was published. Titled *Suzanne Somers' Eat Great, Lose Weight,* it explained her self-developed method for shedding unwanted pounds and keeping them off, which she had researched with nutritionists, books, and trial and error.

Regarding the latter book, she said, "My objective was to find a way to eat healthy, nutritious, yet flavorful foods in substantial portions and still lose weight."

She said the idea had come to her when she had enjoyed a delicious dinner in the home of Frenchman Jean Pierre Fougeriol, who revealed to her the French method of combining foods in a way that created tasty meals without making one feel stuffed.

"The key words to my new way of eating are Eliminate, Separate, and Combine. I eliminate foods like sugar and white flour that wreck havoc on one's system. I separate by grouping foods into proteins and fats, vegetables, carbohydrates, and fruits. And I combine by deciding which of those food can best be eaten together in order to achieve the maximum weight-losing and weight-maintaining results. "

We managed to finish our conversation without my "getting lost."

Chapter 49

Carradine, Berry and The "Next" Generation

David Carradine

I nearly forgot to mention David Carradine in this book because, although Ralph and I spent a few hours with him and his then wife, Gail, at their rural area ranch, I didn't really have an occasion to write a lot about him.

David was a friendly host and I loved seeing his horses, but nothing really memorable came of this visit.

Ken Berry

The reason that Ralph and I found ourselves at the San Fernando Valley home of actor Ken Berry was to photograph and write about his collection of small vintage cars for the Franklin Mint car publication, *Wheels*.

You may know Ken best for his TV roles in *F Troop*, *Mayberry R.F.D.* and *Mama's Family*. He later appeared in *The Golden Girls*. And he was in such movies as *Herbie Rides Again*, *The Cat From Outer Space*, and *Hello, Down There*.

Born in Moline, Illinois, Ken started dancing at the age of 12 and, by the age of 15, he was touring with Big Band Leader and Talent Discoverer Horace Heidt.

He served in the United States Army in the Korean War with the artillery and then in Special Services. His commanding officer was Leonard Nimoy.

His tiny cars included an American 1933 Austin Seven, under 10 feet long, and a Citroen 2CV.

"My Austin seats four, but very snugly," he said. "It's an extremely small car – the kind you see in circuses with lots of clowns popping out – which is the reason it didn't do well in this country. I am only 5'8" tall, but I have to bend down to see out the windshield."

Ken tried to explain to us just why he liked tiny cars.

"I guess it's the kid in me," he said. "These cars seem like toys. They are lots of fun to drive."

The "Next" Generation

I never met Lee Majors or Anthony Quinn, but I did meet and write about their sons – Lee Majors II and Francesco Quinn.

Lee Majors II

I don't really remember much about the Malibu apartment of this then young man except that it was crowded with his varied sports equipment, which included volley balls, footballs, and baseball gloves. That's because Ralph and I spent most of our time with him by the waters of the Pacific on the sand in back of his building.

Of course, one of the things we asked him about was what it felt like to be the son of television's *Six Million Dollar Man*.

"People gave me a hard time about it," he answered. "but I was real mellow and quiet in school. I didn't want to make waves 'cause I wasn't big enough to pound them back."

By that day, it was a different story. He was 6'1" and 185 pounds of muscle. However, he still didn't want to "make waves," although he very much liked to ride his jet ski. In fact, Ralph took several pictures of him doing so. Among other sports he enjoyed was competing at motocross. And he included weight lifting as one of his exercises.

Lee's mother was Kathy Robinson, his father's first wife. Following their divorce, he lived with his mother, and, later, a step-father, in the state of Kentucky, where he attended Eastern Kentucky University and received his Theatre Arts education.

But he had also managed to squeeze in some professional acting experience, appearing in an episode of *The Love Boat* that actually included a trip to Hong Kong.

"I took my Dad along as a guest," he said. "Then, when we returned, he had a show to do in China and he took *me* along as *his* guest, so we had three weeks of traveling together. "

Later, Lee appeared in an episode of his father's other series, *The Fall Guy*, played a supporting role in *The Return of The Six Million Dollar Man and The Bionic Woman* and its sequel, and portrayed his father's son in an episode of *Tour of Duty*.

Francesco Quinn

The sixth born child of his Mexican/Irish/Italian actor father, Anthony Quinn, Frankie (as he was called) was actually one of 12 children, although one of his brothers had died at the tender age of two.

For our meeting, Ralph and I drove to a mountaintop area of

Mulholland drive, overlooking the San Fernando Valley, where the young man -- and many others -- liked to jog.

Although he had already had several important movie roles, in *Platoon, The Dream Runner, Stand Up,* and *Indio* to his credit, he told us that he was equally involved with his hobby of racing motocross and street bikes, and with the designing and marketing of his own line of mountain bikes. He also raced semi-professionally for the American motorcycle manufacturer ATK.

"Acting is a lot of fun and I've lived around it all my life, but it's not necessarily what I've geared my lifelong dreams about. My business is my lifelong dream. I need the creative outlet of acting, but designing my bikes is also a creative outlet. This year, I even designed a line of shoes for my company," he said.

Since we were doing an article on fitness, Frankie talked a lot about the things he did to stay in shape, including his diet and exercise.

"My father taught us a lot about exercise," he remarked. "He always pushed us to be good athletes. Our house in Italy is way in the country. My dad used to have me go for long walks -- about 15 miles – to go to lunch. He'd say 'You run ahead," and I'd say, 'I don't want to run.'

"My father's philosophy was 'Just get up and do it.' I had to go out on my own before I could appreciate it."

Frankie said that besides using a leg machine, a chin-up bar, a dip machine, running, bicycling, and lifting weights, he liked to swim in the pool at his apartment house with a 25-pound dumbbell weight around his waist.

"People say I'm nuts; that I could get a cramp, go down and never come back up," he admitted. "But I wear a quick-release weight belt, so there's no problem."

I found myself hoping that it continued to work.

Chapter 50

Genial George Kennedy

Actor George Kenney struck me as one of the nicest people I ever had the pleasure of interviewing. It was 1996, and he and his wife, Joan, were living in a comfortable Mediterranean style home in Thousand Oaks, a town several miles west of the San Fernando Valley.

When we rang the bell, Joan met us at the door, and George was not far behind. Barefoot and dressed casually in shorts and sport shirt, he led Ralph and me through a wide two-story hallway and made us comfortable at the dining room table. From there, we could enjoy views of flowering plants through large picture windows of the step-down living room on one side and a step-down den on the other. When I commented on this unusual setting, he explained that the room had originally ended with a wall before the second set of steps until he had decided to add on the den.

I quickly learned that George Kennedy was a modest man who would rather talk about his many celebrity friends than himself.

"I'd rather talk about Jimmy Stewart or Henry Fonda than about me. I think the greatest joys of my life have been working with people like them," he said.

It occurred to me that one reason Kennedy was so appreciative of his peers and actors somewhat older was that he came to Hollywood at a more mature age than some.

George was born into a show business family in New York. His mother was a ballet dancer, and his father, a musician and orchestra leader, died when George was only four. George first became a radio performer. During World War II, he joined the Army and received two Bronze Stars as a combat infantryman with General Patton (whom he later portrayed in the 1978 movie *Brass Target*). Talked into re-enlisting, he eventually ended up with the Armed Forces Radio and Television Service.

"I have a curved spine, which had become increasingly troublesome," he told me, "and I spent my last two years in the military either being the technical advisor on "The *Sergeant Bilko* TV show or going to the hospital to be operated on."

He finally retired from the Army and was hired as a civilian technical advisor for that show. He did some acting for them, too, and then became a regular on "*Gunsmoke* and *Have Gun Will Travel.*

Because of his back problem, he told me that he had to strap himself up when he learned to ride a horse by doing so on the bridle trails of Griffith Park. He also found a chiropractor who would put him back in shape when that was needed.

His "name-dropping" continued throughout our interview as he told us more about the fellow actors with whom he had worked.

"John Wayne and I became good friends," he said. "He was larger than life in every sense. He was a very strong man. You could sit talking with him for an hour, but you never forgot you were with *John Wayne*. There was nothing wishy-washy about him. He could be dead wrong, but he was positive he was right.

When you did a picture with him, even if he wasn't directing, he would sometimes suggest how you should say something. Then you would find yourself sounding just like him. That was the danger. He was a very powerful man."

My favorite Kennedy performance was the role of airline troubleshooter Joe Patroni in the 1970 movie *Airport*. When he said he would move a snow-stuck airplane off the crucial runway, I knew that come hell or high water, he was going to do it.

George told me that *his* favorite movie that he worked in was the 1963 *Charade* with Cary Grant and Audrey Hepburn. He said that he and Cary Grant developed a lasting friendship.

Describing Grant as "very meticulous," he told of a scene in which the actor failed to get the effect he wanted.

"He had only to leave Audrey, walk to the elevator and get on. But there was a bit of business he wanted to do with his cuff. Finally, he asked the director for a five minute break. Then, when everyone had left, he walked up and down, doing the scene again and again. When he called everybody back, he did it on the first take."

George had made nearly 100 movies by then and told me that he had portrayed mostly "bad guys" until co-starring with Paul Newman in the 1967 movie *Cool Hand Luke.*

"I was determined to make the most of the opportunity to share a picture with a superstar, so I played to the best of my ability and the chemistry worked. When the picture came out, they saw there were two sides to the coin. It changed everything. After that, 75 percent of the things I got to do were good guys."

An avid reader of books and magazines, George had written a couple of published mystery books. He also enjoyed working at graphic arts on his computer.

"I'm really a very quiet person," he remarked. "At a party, instead of entertaining the crowd, I'll be off in a corner talking with one person. When you put the camera on me and say 'Act,' and I'm playing whatever role it is, then, for that brief period of time I give 110 percent. After that, I prefer to fade into the background."

George and Joan had both been married before and were each the parent of an adopted son and daughter. At the time of our interview, they shared four grandchildren, one of whom – two-year-old granddaughter Taylor -- was living with them due to her mother's substance-abuse problem. Later, they adopted that little girl.

Chapter 51

Bob and Dolores Hope — A Prize-Winning Pair

Although Ralph and I had attempted to arrange an interview with busy Bob Hope regarding what we were told was his collection of golf clubs back in our early days of working for *Collectibles Illustrated*, it wasn't until several years after that publication had closed down that we actually connected with him.

The article we finally produced on Bob was a cover story for the winter 1995 issue of *Mature American,* featuring Bob and his long-time wife Dolores in both the story and the cover picture.

We drove into the Hopes' seven acre Toluca Lake complex of home and offices, and were admitted into the large house.

I must say that I thoroughly enjoyed my resulting conversation with the two of them. As with my interview with Paul Lynde, I found myself talking with two other Gemini people. (Dolores's birthday was May 27 like mine and Bob's was May 29), which I believed help to make us comfortable with each other.

Because Bob's hearing left much to be desired, it was helpful to be talking with both of them as a couple. Together, they proved to be hilarious. And their adoration for each other was cheerfully obvious. Not only that, I quickly learned that Bob had little need of a script writer to make him entertaining. At 91, he was still a marvel at adlibbing.

We sat at a small round table in the large, well-lighted room.

I already knew that Bob had been born in Eltham, England and Dolores was born in Harlem and raised in the Bronx.

"Since your real name was Leslie Townes Hope, how did you happen to choose to be called 'Bob'?" I asked.

He laughed heartily at my unexpected question and said, "I thought it was a *chummy* name."

"Chummier than Leslie," added Dolores. "He didn't want to be called Les Hope. Get it? That's hopeless spelled backwards."

"Kids used to call me Hopeless," chimed in Bob. "I'd chase them for miles --if they were *small* kids."

Bob had moved to Cleveland, Ohio with his parents and six siblings in 1907 and became an American citizen by virtue of the naturalization of his father in 1920. As a teenager, he held a variety of jobs – peddled newspapers, jerked sodas, sold shoes, hustled pool, and served as a delivery boy in his brother Fred's meat market. He also tried his hand at newspaper reporting and at amateur boxing under the name of Packy East.

After graduating from high school, he took dancing lessons and appeared at nearby vaudeville houses with his girlfriend, Mildred Rosequist and later teamed with other male partners. Later, as a single, in 1932, he had a featured role on Broadway in *Ballyhoo*, and, in *1933*, in *Roberta*. It was during the latter period that he met Dolores.

"George Murphy (the late actor/ dancer/senator) was in *Roberta* with me and he introduced us," Bob explained. "One night after the show, he asked me, 'Do you want to hear a pretty girl sing?'

"I said 'Yeah.' So he took me to the Vogue Club.

"Dolores stepped out singing 'Paper Moon' in her low, husky, soft and sweet voice and I said 'Whoops, how long has this been going on?'

"So I started dating her and dating her and dating her."

Once they were married, Bob included Dolores in his vaudeville act.

"We went around the big time circuits together. She'd sing and I'd look starry-eyed and love-struck as she performed. The audiences loved her and so did I."

Bob was proud of the many honors bestowed upon his wife and of the fact that she had recently returned to singing, with three albums to her credit. She was Honorary Mayor of Palm Springs (where they had another home). Other awards included Los Angeles Woman of the Year, Chicago Lady of the Year, Outstanding Mother of the Year, the President's Medal and the Elizabeth Seton Medal Award.

Dolores told me that after children entered the picture, she chose to become a stay-at-home mom. Tony, Linda, Nora and Kelly could never complain that they didn't have a mother around to listen to them. By this time, she and Bob were proud of their four grandchildren.

They also had a family of dogs. Two that we ended up photographing with them were a white Alsatian (also known as German Shepherds) brother and sister pair named Snow Job and Snowelle.

Dolores related a story of the first such pet that started their enthusiasm for that breed.

"We were about to take off from England when a friend brought an Alsatian puppy to the airport," she said, " We got permission to take him with us on the plane. When we changed planes in Chicago, some children asked Bob what the dog's name was and he said, 'My Dog.' So that was what we called him from then on.

Over the 60 years of their marriage to date at that time, Bob had made some 35 movies, received 2,000 awards -- including 54 honorary doctorates -- and traveled the globe to entertain American military troops known as "GIs." He had been dubbed such nicknames as "America's No 1 Soldier in Greasepaint" and "GI Bob."

Dolores accompanied him on some of those trips, including the one to Saudi Arabia during Operation Desert Storm on Christmas of 1991. But most of the time, she kept the home fires burning, waiting patiently for Bob to come home and celebrate their own holiday a few days late. Far from resentful, she insisted it was "just as good."

However, she did admit to some anxious moments, due to the fact that Bob so often placed himself in harm's way. She recalled a close call in Alaska when Bob's plane ran into a storm and lost its radio.

Bob took up that story. "We were very lucky. A tank felt our backwash, reported where we were, and they sent up an anti-aircraft light to guide us down.'

"Another time," remembered Dolores, "his plane made an emergency landing on a sandbar in the vicinity of Australia. When a member of the party stood out, calling for help, a fellow came up in a little boat and asked if they had any American cigarettes."

"Where was that? asked Bob

"Near a town called Lorrington," answered Dolores, after some deliberation.

Bob gazed at her admiringly. "What a memory you have!" he said.

Dolores smiled sweetly. "Don't ever forget it," she retorted.

Chapter 52
Stars I Barely Knew

I spent enough time with most of the stars that I interviewed to feel that I knew them reasonably well. In fact, I often had the occasion to write more than one article about them and deal with a variety of aspects of their lives, talents, and interests. However, there were a few that I spoke to only briefly for one reason or another with but a single story opportunity. Yet, they were famous enough that even a slight acquaintance merited notice. The following represent some of those occasions.

Jack Klugman

Although Jack Klugman has always been one of my favorite actors, my interview with him proved disastrous. It wasn't Jack's fault; he was gracious and fun during the hour or so that we spent talking in his trailer/dressing room at the studio location of his *Quincy, M.E.* TV series.

The fault was not entirely mine, either. It was a hot day and the trailer's air conditioner was bent on keeping us both pleasantly cool.

The problem was that, once I was home again, I found out that the only thing I could hear on the audio tape I had made was that same air conditioner. Had I been wise enough to concentrate more on the details of what was being said, as I did back in the days before I depended on a tape recorder to make note of my information, I could have written the article and fulfilled my assignment for *The Christian Science Monitor*. As it was, I simply failed to produce one.

Margaret O'Brien

I never really thought about meeting former child star Margaret O'Brien, even though I had enjoyed her movies in my own earlier years. We were both a lot older by then and her truly notable days had been back in the 1940s.

My favorite of her movies was *Meet Me in St. Louis,* in which she had co-starred with Judy Garland, who portrayed her older sister. Others had included *Journey for Margaret*, in which she had starred at a mere five-years-old, and *Jane Eyre,* for which she had earned a Special Academy Award as a child actress.

It's been said that Margaret O'Brien (born Angela Maxine O'Brien) was one of the most highly regarded child actors in cinematic history.

The reason that Ralph and I visited Margaret at her San Fernando Valley home was to photograph and write about a new Margaret O'Brien doll, which certainly did resemble her as a child, dark-haired pigtails and all. And it was not the first, since there had been an earlier Margaret O'Brien Doll, by Madame Alexander, back when she was about seven-years-old.

By this time, she was the mother of a 12-year-old daughter of her own.

She told us that, as a child, she had an assortment of dolls, including rag dolls made for her by actor Lionel Barrymore.

But her dolls of that time did not last long. She laughed as she told us why.

"When I made the movie *Bad Bascomb* with Wallace Beery, I played cowboys and Indians and scalped all my dolls. I did such a good job that all those dolls went by the wayside and I had to start collecting all over again.

Linda Blair

Probably still best known for her portrayal as a possessed child in *The Exorcist,* Linda Blair surprised me with her happy but raucous laughter. The grownup Linda was far too dainty and attractive to match that laugh, I thought, but with my own smile of appreciation. You couldn't help but grin along with the good-natured 31-year-old actress.

While visiting at Linda's home, Ralph and I were introduced to a good friend of hers, who helped to produce some of the laughter. It was Murray Langdon, the writer and "The Unknown Comic," who frequently appeared on *The Gong Show*, wearing a brown paper bag over his head and face.

At that time, Linda was helping to publicize her latest movie, *Repossessed,* which was a spoof on *The Exorcist.*

"I think it's hilarious," she said. "I've always wanted to do a comedy, but this is my first major role of that nature. I play a mother whom no one knows was possessed before and I figure out I'm getting repossessed. I turn into a gremlin kind of character – a very obnoxious demon. But it's all in fun."

Actually, she had received a Golden Globe Award, an Oscar nomination and a People's Choice Award at the age of 15 for *The Exorcist*. And, following that, had appeared in a large number of movies.

In addition, she had taken time out to indulge her love of horses by riding hunters and jumpers on the show-ring circuit for a number of years, and was also adept at riding western cutting horses.

Linda has always been known for her love of animals and, to this day, she actively supports animal rights causes.

Tom Poston

Because Tom Poston's wife, Kay Hudson, was coping with Multiple Sclerosis and quite ill at the time of our interview with him, Ralph and I met Tom at an out-of-the-way Beverly Hills park.

Hoping to be inconspicuous, we settled down on a shady bench. However, tour buses, joggers, golfers, and passing motorists all recognized the friendly actor; some even pausing to express their admiration for him. The quietly unassuming gentleman politely exchanged pleasantries and even posed for a picture with one apologetically persistent fan.

Although I knew Tom best for his comedic roles on every successful, long-running *Bob Newhart Show*, he was then playing a recurring role in the ABC comedy series, *Grace Under Fire*. He'd been in several TV series, movies including *Cold Turkey*, and had leads in a number of top Broadway shows.

He said he had specially enjoyed playing the befuddled "Man

on the Street" role on *The Steve Allen Show*.

"Steve and I met and worked with the finest entertainers in the world back then," he said. "We were just kids, having a great time ourselves and loving every minute of it. As long as all I was doing was *The Steve Allen Show*, I thought I was out of work, 'cause it was so much fun."

Tom was truly surprised when he received an Emmy award for that role. "I wasn't even going to attend that event," he told me.

Tom's wife passed away about two years after our visit. Recently, checking on the Internet, I was pleased to learn that a few years later, Tom married a former *Bob Newhart Show* co-star, Suzanne Pleshette. I felt that he deserved to enjoy another happy relationship.

Chapter 53

Janet Leigh was One of My Favorite Actresses

Because I had recently read a novel written by Actress Janet Leigh, entitled *House of Destiny*, I was especially interested in talking with her when Ralph and I paid her a visit at her hilltop Beverly Hills Home in 1995.

I was to learn that it had taken her eight years of research, plotting, and long-hand writing to produce that 500-plus page novel. And she was planning a sequel.

Actually, she had also co-authored another recent book which was a documentary called *Psycho: Behind the Scenes of the Classic Thriller*, with Christopher Nickens. And, in 1984 had written her autobiography entitled *There Really Was a Hollywood*, which I had read many years before.

Although, at that time, she already had nearly 50 motion pictures to her credit, Janet seemed to be best known for her role in Alfred Hitchcock's horror movie *Psycho*. However, my favorite of her movies was *Bye Bye Birdie*, in which she co-starred with the teenage Ann-Margret, Dick Van Dyke, Paul Lynde and Maureen

Stapleton. And I also enjoyed the funny *Hello Down There*. But, of course, it was difficult to choose, since her movies included dramas, westerns, comedies and musicals.

She said that if she had to choose her favorites it would probably be the historical movies. "It was fun pretending that you were living at that time, with all the clothes, the props and the settings."

Janet told me that she was not at all insulted when she was referred to as the mother of Jamie Lee Curtis or Kelly Curtis. She recalled with fondness the first time that happened many years before.

"I was car-pooling to pick up my kids at school and when my turn in line came, someone called out, 'Here's Jamie and Kelly's mom.' I loved it then and I still do."

About the movie *Psycho*, she said, "I co-authored the book about it with Christopher Nickens. I wanted to correct some of the misconceptions the public had about my work in that film. For instance, it was said that Mr. Hitchcock ordered that the water in the shower murder scene be cold to help me express shock. I'm certainly a good enough actress that I didn't need that. Actually, it was comfortably warm."

She smiled. "And, yes, it was me in all the shower scenes, but I wasn't completely naked. Parts of me were covered with flesh-colored moleskin."

Although some other actresses had complained of finding Mr. Hitchcock too demanding, Janet said it hadn't been that way with her. "By the time I did *Psycho*, I had already made 32 pictures and had had my name above the title, so it wasn't as if I were someone he'd discovered and was trying to promote. He was not my Svengali."

And, after having made that movie, she said she really did prefer tub baths to showers.

While Ralph and I had been with Janet, we had also been enjoying the company of her two dogs –Sara, a Black Lab, and Joe, a Golden Retriever, which she called "my babies., saying "If my dogs want to get up on the couch, I don't care. I don't want a room where nobody ever sits on the furniture. What's the use of that?"

Born Jeanette Helen Morrison on July 6, 1927 in Merced, California, Janet had the retired actress Norma Shearer to thank for her movie career. Impressed with a picture of the pretty young girl on the desk of her parents, who were employed at the ski lodge she visited, Ms. Shearer asked for a copy which she passed around to her Hollywood friends. The result was a contract with MGM and a new name for Jeanette.

Even in her busiest acting days and her marriage to actor Tony Curtis, the father of her two daughters, Janet's priorities placed her children and her husband ahead of her career.

Married in 1951, Janet and Tony were divorced in 1962. Still, she agreed to tell us some things about him.

"I met him at a press party. He was a devastatingly handsome young man with black unruly hair, large sensitive eyes fringed by dark lashes, a full sensitive mouth, and an irresistible personality.

"When he phoned to ask me for a date, he did it with the voice of Cary Grant, which was a favorite imitation he learned to do while on a submarine during World War II, watching the movie *Gunga Din* -- the only film on board -- over and over." She laughed. "Of course I realized who he really was, so I went along with the gag and told him that I'd be delighted to go out with him, but I already had an engagement that night with Tony Curtis."

During their marriage, they co-starred in six feature films and traveled extensively.

"Tony and I had good times together," she recalled. "We had wonderful years. And we have two beautiful children. But we began to go in different directions."

At this time, they shared an eight-year-old granddaughter, Annie, the child of Jamie Lee and her husband.

By then, Janet had been married to stockbroker Robert Brandt for 33 years. Having told us about her first impressions of Tony Curtis, she did the same regarding her current husband.

"I found him funny, well mannered, very intelligent, warm, sexy, strong, practical, realistic, steady, private, and disarmingly naïve, in regard to my profession especially," she said.

I found Janet to be as warm, friendly and likeable as I had always perceived her to be in the many movies of hers that I had enjoyed. She was also prone to counting her blessings.

"I've been so fortunate," she remarked. "It just seemed that life smiled on me. I was discovered for the acting business and I tried to learn everything that I could. It was never a chore. And now, to have my life open up to this writing, which I adore, I just feel so fulfilled, and I am deeply grateful."

Chapter 54

Our Visit with Orson Bean

Do you think Orson Bean is a funny name? You should, because that is what it was intended to be and was not the real name of the man who claims it. The actor using that name was born Dallas Frederick Burrows. His father, George Frederick Burrows was co-founder of The American Civil Liberties Union and a cousin to Calvin Coolidge, who was the United States President in 1928, the year that Dallas Burrows was born.

Dallas Burrows took the name of Orson Bean when, as a young magician and comic, he found it helped to get him more laughs than did being introduced by his real name.

When Ralph and I drove down to the venerable southern California town of Venice, California to pay him a visit, he was Orson Bean and had been for some 50 years. And, of course, on the *Dr. Quinn, Medicine Woman* television series (starring Jane Seymour) he was storekeeper Loren Bray.

As we parked the car and walked down the lane leading to his house (which was actually two side-by-side smallish houses linked together by a sunlit walkway) I realized that he was the only person I had ever known who lived along one of the man-made canals in that town.

While I was marveling at this, a flock of large white geese were marveling at me. To my dismay, they decided that I was truly fascinating and decided to swarm about me to pay their respects – or, more likely, to attack me, I discovered. Trying to escape, I appealed to Ralph to drive them away, since they had no interest in him. Instead, my long-time business partner chose to pull out his camera and proceed to photograph my dilemma, laughing all the while.

By the time we located Orson's house, I was not in a good mood to undertake an interview, but I soon pulled myself together.

I had recently read his autobiography, *Too Much Is Not Enough* (copyright 1988) and had been fascinated by an experience he had related about making friends with a Monarch butterfly while living in a house in Pacific Palisades. When Orson talked to it, the orange and black butterfly had actually landed on his finger, held onto it with its little legs, and opened and closed its wings. It came back frequently for a period of two weeks to spend time with him before continuing on the migration (south in winter; north in summer) for which the Monarchs are famous in America. For the next few years, many Monarch butterflies paid visits to the property so long as the family continued to live there.

I talked about that with Orson, who enjoyed discussing it with me.

Orson's credits included radio, Broadway shows, movies, and television. Among other Broadway shows, he'd had a starring role in the original cast of *Will Success Spoil Rock Hunter?* in 1955, and was also featured in *Subways Are For Sleeping*.

He'd appeared on television game shows of the 1960s, 1970s, and 1980s, and been a longtime panelist on *To Tell the Truth*. He had been a guest on *The Tonight Show* with both Jack Paar and Johnny Carson.

Orson Bean's philosophy of life seemed to me to be summed up in a story he told me about his role in the *Dr. Quinn* show.

He began by telling me that he had never been interested in doing a TV series due to the long hours of waiting around that are known to be involved in that sort of work.

"But on hearing about that show, I figured I had reached the point where I was old enough and relaxed enough to be able to do it and enjoy it," he explained.

"When I went over to the casting office to read for the part," he continued, "I went to the men's room, got down on my knees, and made a little prayer to be allowed to do a good audition. I didn't pray to get the part. I didn't even know if I wanted it. But I wanted to do a good audition.

"So I did a *great* audition. They called me back the next day to audition a second time, which was a good sign. Again, I went and prayed in the john to be allowed to do a good audition. And I *did* a good audition. I made the people laugh, and I thought, 'These people are going to offer me the part and I'm going to have to decide whether to do it or not.'

"But my agent called and said, 'The show's executive producer and creator, Beth Sullivan, is dying to have you, but the CBS guys say you're too old. So you didn't get the part.'

"I said, 'All right. My prayers were answered. I did a good audition. Whether or not I got the part was not my business. That was God's business.'

"A few months later, I heard that CBS had made the pilot and they didn't like the guy that they hired. So apparently Beth Sullivan said, 'Well, give me the one I wanted in the first place,' and I wound up getting the part.

"What I learned from that is when stuff is supposed to happen, it happens, and when it isn't, it doesn't, and that's not your business. Your business is to do what's in front of you, which, in this case, was the audition.

"So I got the part and I've had it for five years, and I love going up there to that wonderful spot where we shoot it."

Location for the show was the Paramount Ranch, with open country, live oak trees and a small old-western town, in Agoura Hills – no more than an hour's drive from Orson's home.

Also picturesque was Orson's own neighborhood. Deep blue morning glories and white oleander sprawled over the land side of his property and another array of colorful flowers adorned the deck overlooking the waterway. Each quaintly different house in view had its own little dock and boat.

"When my grandchildren come to visit, we take them out in our boat," he remarked.

A longtime resident, Orson had seen many changes in his personal life since moving to the area. Divorced from his second wife, Carolyn, he stayed on in the house alone for about a dozen years before meeting and marrying actress Alley Mills.

Chapter 55

They Had the Wizard of Oz in Common

The "Almost Scarecrow"

First, I am going to tell you about Buddy Ebsen – the man who very nearly became a cast member of the 1939 movie, *The Wizard of Oz*, but lost out through no fault of his own.

Although Buddy Ebsen had been asked to play the Scarecrow in *The Wizard of Oz* , it seems that Ray Bolger, who had been chosen to play the Tin Woodsman, really wanted that part. So Buddy generously agreed to switch. All would have been well had not the makeup people goofed when they attempted to illustrate his "tin-ness." Their initial idea was to coat his body with aluminum dust. Buddy, unknowingly, inhaled the stuff into his lungs and became seriously ill. While he lay recovering, the part of the Tin Woodsman was given to Jack Haley, who benefited by the makeup being changed to a less harmful silver paste.

And, as agreed, Ray Bolger became the Scarecrow. And Buddy Ebsen lost any chance of appearing in the movie that was to become a classic.

Buddy Ebsen wrote about that experience in his 1993 autobiography, *The Other Side of Oz.*

*It was i*n 1998 that I visited Buddy Ebsen at his Palos Verde, California home. I was on assignment to *Collector's Mart* magazine to write about the series of amusing oil paintings Mr. Ebsen (then 90yearsold) had painted of Jed Clampett and family, characters from his 1962 – 1971 TV series, *The Beverly Hillbillies.* The pictures were being reproduced as signed and numbered prints and canvas transfers. They included such scenes as Jed with his dog and cabin, Jed bringing home a Christmas tree, and Jed with a variety of farm animals called his "critters." There would be 10 in all and each one featured Buddy's signature mark– a small red cardinal, his favorite bird.

Instead of going with Ralph, I rode out there with the photographer assigned by the magazine. Buddy and I sat at the table in his sun-filled Breakfast Room and talked about many things.

"I was born in Belleville, Illinois, but my family moved to Orlando, Florida for my mother's health," he told me. "She herself painted, and it was so beautiful there that she signed up all us kids to take art lessons. "

He said that he was taking pre-med classes at Rollins College when his family fell on hard times, making it necessary for him to drop out. With a father who ran a dancing school, he was already an experienced "hoofer," so he went to New York to try his luck at turning "pro."

Buddy performed in a number of Broadway shows including *Ziegfeld Follies* and many films, including *Captain January* with child actress Shirley Temple, and *Breakfast at Tiffany's* with Audrey Hepburn. He also served as "sidekick" to Fess Parker's *Davy*

Crocket. Following *The Beverly Hillbillies,* he starred in the detective series *Barnaby Jones.*

Always interested in boats, Buddy served with the United States Coast Guard during World War II. In 1968, he won the transpacific catamaran race from Los Angeles to Honolulu on his 35 foot catamaran, *Polynesian Concept.* He wrote a book about that experience named after his boat, and also wrote a novel entitled *Kelly's Quest.*

The Man Who *Became* The Scarecrow

Ralph and I had visited the large white Beverly Hills house of Ray Bolger back in the 1980s on assignment to *Collectibles Illustrated.* Actually, our interview took place in Ray's office, which we reached by following a long, narrow sidewalk past his sunny rose garden (bordered with strawberries and carrots), past the swimming pool and under the shade of an enormous avocado tree.

The reason for our visit had to do with his role as the Scarecrow, for an issue featuring *Wizard of Oz* collectibles. So that is what we talked about.

He explained why he had refused the Tin Woodsman part he had initially been assigned and insisted on the Scarecrow role.

"The Tin Woodsman part wasn't my cup of tea," he explained. "My style was more fluid."

Even after Buddy Ebsen began his costume fittings for the role of the Scarecrow, Ray continued to insist that he had been miscast and he somehow managed to wear his bosses down

Ray told us that he was happy in his triumph, but he, also, had to deal with an unusual costume. His Scarecrow makeup took two hours to apply. It consisted of a rubber bag, wrinkled to simulate burlap, which covered his entire head except for his facial features. The bag was glued to his head daily; then brown makeup was blended over the center of his face to match. Hand-painted lines about nose and mouth continued the burlap effect. Ray was to find that he had acquired permanent lines about his mouth and chin, due to the months of wearing his Scarecrow face.

Because he also had to wear heavy underwear to protect himself from the scratchiness of the straw in his costume, and dance under the heat of "every unused arc light in Hollywood," he actually fainted a couple of times. But this was considered a fairly common occurrence among the actors on that set.

Regarding a scene that Ray said was cut from the original, due to its quality being out of proportion to other numbers, and only shown at a later date in a documentary movie called *That's Dancing!*, Ray said, "I flew through the air on wires, chasing crows away from the cornfields, bounced against the fence on the Yellow Brick Road from one side to the other, and did a split which I couldn't get out of. After they edited it, there were just a couple of steps and a fall left in."

One of Ray's favorite special effects occurred when the flying monkeys tore the Scarecrow apart and scattered his straw all about, invoking his line, "That's me all over."

"Actually, " he explained, "I was down in a hole with just my head sticking out."

Ralph and I had greatly enjoyed our visit with the warm and friendly 79-year-old gentleman who summed up his thoughts on the topic as follows.

"To me," he said emphatically, "*The Wizard of Oz* is a great

American classic, and, long after I'm gone, it will be and I will be remembered as the Scarecrow. It's a wonderful thing to have a memory, especially when it's a memory you're proud of. Have I got a memory? You bet your life I have -- *The Wizard of Oz!*"

Chapter 56

Stars on the Phone

Depending on the job and the sort of article I was writing, I sometimes resorted to telephone interviews; in that case using one or another methods of taping my interview for accuracy. But it was a rare occasion for my celebrity interviews, as I much preferred to meet with them on a face-to-face basis. The following are examples of those occasions with explanations of why they were necessary.

Jasmine Guy

There was no other way for me to interview Jasmine Guy as she was in New York at the time I needed to speak with her. The odd thing was that I was doing the story for *Woman's World* magazine, which is located in that area.

Jasmine was portraying Whitley Gilbert – the one she termed "the bad guy" – on the TV series called *A Different World*, which was a spin-off from *The Cosby Show*. It starred Lisa Bonet as the Huxtables' second-oldest daughter, Denise, gone off to college.

"I thought everybody would hate Whitley," she told me, "but now they are trying to develop the other sides of the characters."

For hers, it meant allowing her to show empathetic and sympathetic aspects that helped viewers to relate in a positive manner, earning her the nickname of "the black Scarlett O'Hara."

Jasmine told me that she was the daughter of a black minister and a white school teacher who met during their Boston school days. She was born in Boston and raised in Atlanta. Her family stressed education and she was allowed to take ballet and perform so long as she kept her grades up. At the age of 17, she left home to study at the Alvin Alley Dance Center. By the time of our interview, she had a number of Broadway and television credits.

I regretted that I never had the opportunity to meet her in person.

Danny Aiello

As with Jasmine, Danny Aiello was in New York when I had the privilege of speaking with him for an article in a publication called *Active Times*. He was producing and starring in a television series called *Dellaventura*, which was about a New York private investigator, based on the true exploits of a former New York detective. Among other movie roles, he had portrayed Cher's jilted fiancé in *Moonstruck* and played Sal in Spike Lee's *Do the Right Thing*.

He told me about his 43-year-marriage to his wife, Sandy, his close relationship to their four sons and one daughter, and his seven grandchildren.

"I think that the compassionate sensitivity I have toward others originated partially because I was nurtured by five women – four sisters and my mother, with no father at home," he said.

Having also portrayed Jack Ruby, in the feature film, *Ruby,* about the murderer of Lee Harvey Oswald – the man who killed President Kennedy -- he said that movie critics Gene Siskel and Roger Ebert, said he did it as "too nice of a guy."

"But Jack Ruby was loved by a lot of people," he explained, "and the fact was that he loved Jack Kennedy and thought he was the savior of the Jewish people. Even the most vicious of killers – when he's not killing -- may be hugging his mother."

Maureen O'Sullivan

I have to say that it was, indeed, a thrill to speak with this lovely Irish lady, who was known as "Ireland's first film star," even though it was just a phone interview because she was "back east" somewhere.

After all, she had been the co-star of Johnny Weissmuller, playing Jane to his Tarzan in the days when my cousin Joyce and I had been excited to attend that series of movies and act them out in Joyce's big yard. By that time, along with her own many movie credits, she was also known as the mother of actress Mia Farrow.

My purpose was to write about her personal holiday memories for the 1987 Christmas issue of *The Franklin Mint Almanac*. She obliged beautifully and I only wish I had space here to relate the entire conversation.

Maureen was born in Boyle, County Roscommon, Ireland in 1911. She told me that, at the age of six, she and her family were living with her grandfather in his "wonderful old Georgian house in western Ireland" while her father recuperated from wounds acquired in the first World War.

She said that there was no electricity or gas there, only light from oil lamps and candles. And she talked about the bogs beneath the window of the nursery she shared with her four-year-old brother, where hundreds of tiny lights twinkled, and how the children believed they were faeries -- the little people -- although "cynical people" always said it was just phosphorous.

"Christmas was a magical time," she recalled. "To add to the enchantment, on the night before Christmas, my grandfather would have his groom drive his team of horses round and round the house, so that we would hear the sounds of the hoofs and the bells he would ring and think it was Father Christmas coming to see us.

"We went to bed in great anticipation. We knew that sometime in the night – after the fire in the fireplace had died down – Father Christmas would come right into our room and fill the stockings we had hung at the foot of our beds. When we awoke, there would be toys on the bed and on the floor and we'd see the Christmas tree which had been decorated for us after we were asleep."

She told me about one especially beautiful doll for her and a special Teddy bear for her younger brother.

"One thing puzzled me at that time," she concluded. "Why were the things my parents chose to give me not at all the glamorous sort of treats that Father Christmas brought to me? It was to be many years before I realized that this illusion was, perhaps, the greatest gift of all."

Chapter 57

Born in the 1920'S

The following three actors all shared the 1920s as their birthdates, and were all favorites of mine during my own earlier years. I am telling about them here alphabetically.

Turhan Bey

Although fans considered Turhan Bey handsome enough to play leading man roles during his 1940s to early 1950s Hollywood career, he told me his favorite part was that of a boy whose job it was to take care of the mummy in the movie *The Mummy's Tomb*.

"I always enjoyed playing character roles and interesting 'heavies' or villains," said the Turkish/Jewish/Czech actor-turned-photographer. "I was never really comfortable playing a leading man."

Ralph and I met with him at the Beverly Hills home of one of his old friends, which he used as a headquarters when visiting Los Angeles from his own home in Vienna.

I learned that his real full name was Turhan Gilbert Selahattin Schultavey.

Born in Austria in 1922, he originally came to the United States in 1940 after Nazi Germany took over that country. In California, he joined a drama class, hoping to improve his English and was discovered by talent scouts while playing a weird character in his first stage play.

"I was given the part of an Indian servant in an Errol Flynn picture called *Footsteps in the Dark.*"

Turhan made a large number of movies, co-starring with Katharine Hepburn, Merle Oberon, Gloria Grahame, and Maria Montez. His movies included *Dragon Seed, Raiders of the Desert, Arabian Nights,* and *Ali Baba and the Forty Thieves.*

When offered a part that he considered beneath his status, he objected, and his contract was sold to a smaller studio.

"If I had been wise, I would have taken that part," he said, "It was written for Peter Lorre and would have put me back into the field I loved best – interesting character roles."

Jimmy Lydon

Like most people of my generation, I knew James "Jimmy" Lydon from his role of Henry Aldrich in *The Aldrich Family* motion picture series about a typical, middle-class, happily adjusted family. Although he was portraying a teenager, Jimmy was actually 23-years-old at the time.

When Ralph and I visited the then 66-year-old actor, he had long before branched out into the fields of directing and producing such television series as *77 Sunset Strip, Wagon Train, McHale's Navy* and *M*A*S*H* , and feature films including *An American Dream* and *Countdown.*

Jimmy told us he had become an actor at the age of 10 out of sheer necessity. He was the fifth in a family of nine children living in Manhattan during depression years.

"My father was a very tortured man and an alcoholic," he explained. "He worked for a giant corporation in the financial district and made a good deal of money.

"One day he came home and sat at our huge dining room table, looked at this big family he had and said, 'I've worked for this family for 18 years and I will never work again.' He didn't retire. He just stopped. My oldest brother was 18. We all scrambled to do whatever we could to keep the family afloat. My mother was devastated. When a friend of hers who had two children in the theater suggested she do the same with one of her children, I was the one chosen."

Jimmy was eventually given a part in a Broadway play.

"I was scared to death. I didn't know anything about acting," he confessed. "The older actors were teaching me my craft as I went along, which was the tradition in those days."

He said did play after play, about 200 radio shows during the 1930s, and later, became "the only child then under contract to RKO Studio." His early films included *Little Men* and Tom Brown's School Days.

Mickey Rooney

I almost said that Mickey Rooney was a "senior citizen" when I finally got to meet him. But scratch that! On the day I did meet him in a hotel lobby in Westlake Village, west of the San Fernando Valley, he emphatically told me that he did not like that term.

He told me that he was starting an organization called Mickey

Rooney's Fun-time Family for people over 45 up to 145. He described all the fun things they would do. Whether or not this ever came to be, I do not know, but it sounded good to me.

"I just turned 75," he said, "so I'm the equivalent of three 25 year old men. The energy, the enthusiasm, and the creativity are the things that keep us all buoyant and forever anticipatory of tomorrow and what tomorrow can bring. People don't have to be old unless they decide to be old. The thought structure that men and women want to look out for is 'I'm too old to do that.' And you'll get other people who say 'I used to be able to do that,' or 'I remember...'

"Don't remember. Get up and do it!"

Mickey's optimism was catching.

The more he talked to me, the more I realized just why I had always enjoyed his acting so much. My only regret was that I had not had the opportunity to become a friend of his.

By then he had been married to his eighth wife, Jan, for 21 years

"She's a lovely girl and my friend," he said. "She's probably one of the best singers in the world. She has five octaves and was a professional singer before I married her."

Mickey said he had no special favorites out of his vast number of accomplishments.

"To be in this business is my favorite gift in life, no matter how infinitesimal or how big the role is. God has been more than good to me with the opportunities he's given me," he said,

From the *Andy Hardy* series, to *Boys Town*, *National Velvet* with the young Elizabeth Taylor, and all his song-and-dance movies with singer-dancer-actress Judy Garland, and right up to the 2006 comedy movie *Night At The Museum*, I must say, I, Shirley, have enjoyed them all.

Chapter 58
Taylor and Holliman

Rod Taylor

Although Rod Taylor starred in several big films and had featured roles in numerous others since the 1950s, when he migrated from his native Australia to the United States of America, fans still tend to identify him with the 1960 science fiction movie *The Time Machine*.

That includes me, though I also do the same with Alfred Hitchcock's *The Birds*, which I still think of as a very good, if very scary, movie.

In fact, that movie was one of the things we talked about when Ralph and I visited him and his Japanese-American wife, Carol, in their two-story English colonial hillside Beverly Hills house.

First he told me a bit about working with Hitchcock. While shooting a scene with Jessica Tandy (who played his mother), Rod noticed that there was no light in the refrigerator on the kitchen set.

"I called to the cameraman, 'Hey, Bobby, don't forget to put a light in the refrigerator.' Whereupon, Hitchcock said, in front of a bunch of visiting journalists, 'We will now take a two-hour lunch break while Mr. Taylor, our technical advisor, tells us how to make our movie.'

"So we had our lunch break and came back and worked the rest of the day. Then Hitchcock had all the press up to his bungalow for cocktails. He sent his secretary, Peggy, down to see me. She said, 'Hitch would love you to come and have cocktails with him.' So I went up and there he was with a space left next to him on the sofa just for me. And he said, 'Here is Rod – my magnificent star.' That was Hitchcock."

As his co-star, Tippi Hedren, had told me, "That movie was a pain to make, and you can take that literally. I'd stick my hands through the shutters and they'd throw seagulls at me and they'd peck the heck out of me. Tippi almost had a nervous breakdown. They put birdseed in her hair and encouraged the birds to 'attack' her."

The first article we did on Rod was a cover story for the fall 1994 issue of *Mature American* magazine.

I learned that it had been approximately 10 years before that when he had become an American citizen.

"It was about time I paid tribute to my new homeland," he said. "I had been living here and working here and owning property here for 30 years. I'm proud to be a citizen."

Rod was 65 at that time and called himself "an old guy." Nevertheless, he was keeping busy with a number of activities. He was helping to design and build his own new 5,000 square-foot, two-story Cape Cod house overlooking the Pacific Ocean near Santa Barbara. He pumped iron when preparing for a movie, golfed ("badly"), played tennis, surfed, ran along the beach, and created a variety of artwork. His house was filled with his own paintings, handmade furniture, and decorative plates.

He said that, back in Australia, after listening to soap operas on the radio, he decided he could be a radio actor, so he auditioned and, he said, "After two years, I was the biggest radio actor in Australia."

From there, he went into the theater .At the age of 24, after playing an 80-year-old blind man in a movie called *Long John Silver*, he was sent for by Warner Bros.. Once he was in California, he was signed to a long-term contract by Metro-Goldwyn-Mayer Studios.

Rod and his first wife, Mary Hilem, were divorced after just five years of marriage, but they shared a daughter, Felicia. Rod told me that she was the anchor woman on the financial network, CNBC in New York.

Earl Holliman

If you watched the *Police Woman* TV series, starring Angie Dickinson, you'll recognize actor Earl Holliman as her co-star, Officer Bill Crowley, Earl's many movie credits include *Forbidden Planet, Gunfight At The O.K. Corral, The Bridges of Toko-Ri,* and *The Rainmaker.*

But, locally, in the Los Angeles area and his San Fernando Valley home, he's known as an animal activist and the long-time president of a philanthropic organization called Actors and Others For Animals.

Appropriately, Ralph and I found his Spanish style house to be situated on a very large park-like, tree filled yard where we sat to talk and take pictures.

Pigeons, doves, squirrels, "rescued" dogs and cats, "cute little tree rats, and an occasional wild rabbit lived and/or visited happily throughout the property, secure in the knowledge that Earl would supply a huge bagful of food for their daily breakfast and dinner.

With so many birds around, he told us that he was thinking of naming his place "Thorn Birds," in honor of the mini-series of that name in which he had co-starred. In fact he already had a wrought-iron sign of that name.

He explained how that came about.

"During the first scene in which I appeared, there were two workmen welding something. We did the scene several times and at the end of the day, one of the welders came up to me and said, 'I don't know what to do with this, so I thought I might as well give it to you.'"

Earl grinned as he exhibited the sign. "He had written 'The Thorn Birds' in metal. So it became a great souvenir of that show and that experience for me. I am thinking of putting it on a wall of my house or over the gate leading into my yard."

I'm sorry to say that I have never checked back to see if that happened.

Regarding his *Police Woman* experience, Earl said, "I wasn't sure I wanted to be in a series with that sort of name, but Angie and I had a wonderful chemistry between us and it turned out to be the smartest move I ever made. To research the part, I spent many nights in the back seat of a black-and-white police car, witnessing the action. And, during the run of the series, I scarcely made a move on the set without checking its authenticity."

Chapter 59
My Jack Palance Run-Around

I was intrigued when I read in a film encyclopedia that Jack Palance crashed in a bomber he was piloting in World War II and was burned so severely that he required plastic surgery. This, it said, resulted in giving his facial features the gaunt, taut-skinned look for which he was famous.

Since, to my knowledge, this was a little-known fact that had never been publicized, I hoped to be able to bring myself to ask him about it. I'm generally timid about approaching sensitive subjects with people, so I made up my mind that, if it bothered him, I'd agree not to write about it.

Equally interesting to me was the fact that he was the son of a Pennsylvania coal miner and had actually worked briefly in the mines himself. He'd also been a school athlete, a professional boxer, and a stage actor before ending up in Hollywood. Portraying the "heavy" in a number of films, he was nominated for an Oscar as best supporting player for *Sudden Fear* in 1952 and for *Shane* in 1953.

He did some TV, including his *Believe It Or Not* series, which he co-hosted with his daughter, Holly. And his vast number of movies was impressive and included the off-beat *Baghdad Café*. Most recently, of course, at this time, was *City Slickers*, the movie which had catapulted him into a new period of fame and won him the Oscar for Best Supporting Actor. And there was additional notice paid when he accepted the honor by performing a number of one-handed push-ups, belying his 73 years.

I'd done my homework well, and was prepared for our promised meeting, which had been arranged by Ralph, who had already met and photographed him a while back for a book entitled *Actors As Artists*.

Although we were under assignment to do two very diverse articles on Palance, neither hinged upon his new-found popularity. One was for a car collectors' publication published by the Franklin Mint. The other was for a cover story for *Mature American* magazine.

"We're all set to photograph Jack's antique cars on Tuesday," Ralph told me over the phone on Friday night. We'll drive out to his ranch early in the morning and be back sometime in the afternoon."

"To his ranch? I thought we were going to his house in Beverly Hills," I countered.

"We'll do that next week," Ralph explained. "This is just to photograph him with his cars. Next week we'll do more pictures at his house and you can do your main interview with him then. On Tuesday you can get your information regarding the cars."

The drive out to the rural area of Tehachapi, just outside the desert town of Mojave, in Ralph's GMC Jimmy, took longer than we'd expected, but it was still only mid-morning when we arrived.

"Jack owns a farm in Pennsylvania," remarked Ralph. "He keeps some of his antique cars back there and some here. He's had this place about 25 years. It has around a thousand acres, and it's named Hollybrook Farm for Jack's two daughters. His son, Cody, lives here in one of those three little houses, and Jack spends quite a bit of time here, too. He has a studio in the barn where he does his oil paintings."

We were driving among live-oak dotted, rolling hills, and, as we neared the small bungalows, came upon a couple of very out-of-place curiosities that caught and held my interest.

"What in the world are those things doing here?" I asked.

Standing a few yards apart from each other were a 15 foot tall winged horse made entirely of gleaming chrome and a 10 foot tall white Leghorn rooster.

Ralph had informed me that Jack had something going on here today, but we'd expected to have our visit with him early and be out of the way. Unfortunately, the "something going on" turned out to be the taping of an introductory narration by Jack for opening scenes of *Legends of the West*, an upcoming television series. At the moment, we learned, he was in a meeting in one of the houses with members of the production company. He'd be out soon.

"Soon" dragged into more than an hour. Wandering about, we spotted some of the vintage cars under protective covers and assumed that others were housed in the barn.

Luckily, to pacify me, Ralph took my picture with the chrome horse. Today, it's the only visible proof that I was ever there.

At last, Jack emerged from the house. Leaving his visitors behind, he ambled over and shook hands with me as Ralph introduced us. This man was tall – 6 ft. 4 inches to my 5 ft. 2.

"What's the story about the chrome horse?" I unwisely asked in the course of our brief conversation. Unwisely because, as I was to realize later, I should have been checking on the things I really needed to know for my articles.

Jack smiled in his own leering way. "The Pegasus? It's made

completely out of car bumpers. It was made by a guy named Josh Gutierrez. I saw it at a Beverly Hills art exhibit, liked it, and bought it."

"And the chicken?"

Again the smile and even a chuckle. "That was a birthday present from my wife. It's made of Fiberglas."

Ralph was uncovering the cars. "They're pretty dusty," he said disapprovingly. "Can you get someone to hose them down so they'll look better in the pictures?"

"Oh sure. Later on. Right now we're going to break for pizza. Then we're going to run over to do some taping. But, after that…"

Before we knew it, he'd gone back to his associates and we were left staring at each other with open mouths.

We gave up for the moment and entered the house to find Cody and some of his rugged looking cowboy friends scattered among the more neatly attired members of the TV crew. They were all filling their plates from what seemed to be dozens of huge open pizza boxes. Never one to turn down free food, I helped myself.

The setting was anything but elegant, but it *was* interesting. I ogled bits of memorabilia Jack had acquired over the years. Prominently displayed was a western saddle I was told that Jack had used when he was playing the bad guy in the movie, *Shane*.

I also learned that one of these small houses had served as a way-station for cowboys driving cattle between Los Angeles and Bakersfield around a hundred years before.

When the crew and Palance drove over to their taping site, Ralph and I decided to follow. A couple of hills away, out of sight of the house, we parked and walked up closer to watch. With cameras rolling, Jack – mounted on a cowpony – drove a small herd of cattle up the hill…over and over again.

Eventually, he dismounted to sit under a tree by a campfire

with a pot of coffee. It was there that he gave his spiel…over and over again.

Anyone who has ever watched a taping knows that it takes long, boring hours. In this case, we were not only uncomfortable standing around the uninviting desert-like hillside; we were anxious to get on with our reason for being there.

At last the time came when everyone headed back to the house area. There was time for Ralph to snap a few pictures of our host with his cars. But there was no time left for me to do any sort of interview.

"We'll talk at my house next week, Shirley," promised Jack. And with that I had to content myself.

As agreed upon, I phoned Jack to set it up, but he seemed reluctant to commit. Another week went by and time was running out. At this point, I told him I'd be willing to settle for a phone interview. Jack was okay with that.

"Call me at 9 a.m. Thursday," he responded.

I knew he had several vintage Fords and Al Capone's 1938 Cadillac. I'd ask about the cars, get some anecdotes, and save that story, regardless of the personality profile cover story, which seemed, by now, almost impossible to pull off.

An early riser, on Thursday I waited impatiently for the agreed-upon hour. I dialed the phone. "Good morning, Jack," I forced myself to say brightly.

"Oh, Shirley," was his greeting. "I'm so sorry, but, you know, I really don't want to do this. I just don't want to be interviewed."

Flabbergasted, I stammered and stuttered. "But I only need you to give me a little information. Just a few facts and remarks about your antique cars."

"I know, but I just don't feel that I want to do it. I hope you'll understand. Okay?"

There seemed nothing left to say but "Okay."

I hung up and phoned his long-time publicist.

"I'm sorry," he said. "I don't know what's gotten into him. But I can't help you. He fired me a couple of days ago."

I conferred by phone with Ralph. "Without some sort of definite information and a few quotes from Jack about the cars, there's no way I can produce a saleable article," I told him.

So that was the end of it. And though it was a big disappointment in more ways than one (including the loss of about a thousand dollars apiece), I still liked Jack Palance.

In some ways, my real life experience with him seemed comparable to that of the city slickers with the ruggedly independent Curly. True, he did, indeed, give me the run-around, but with a style and a lack of malice that I couldn't help but admire.

Chapter 60
Stars Who Loved the Ocean

Here are some of the stars I interviewed who had special reasons for their attraction to the Pacific Ocean.

Ed Asner

I met actor Ed Asner through my association with Hollywood Women's Press Club and finally had an occasion to write an article about him. It was an as-told-to article, in which he described what his seashell collection meant to him for *The Franklin Mint Almanac*.

You may recall what I consider my favorite role of his, Lou Grant on *The Mary Tyler Moore Show*.

I drove to his private office outside of Hollywood and admired his "treasures."

He talked about the years when he and his former wife would rent a beach house for the summer when their children were young.

"Late in the afternoon, when the beach had been combed by us and by everybody else, we'd go out to the last line, as the water receded, and grab up a handful of 'clutter,' which would turn out to be tiny specimens of all the big shells. There'd be whelks, sand dollars, sea buttons, coffee beans, and apple stars."

He said that, other times, they'd drive down to the beach from town for a couple hours of "shelling."

"Oddly, we fell in love with a shell that's one of the most primitive order found – the Chilton. Bluish in color, they have the form of butterfly wings. We were fascinated by them until we found out that they belonged to the ugly animal that covered the rocks off the coast. You'll find them all over the world – the lowly Barnacle."

Ed also collected fossils, when he could find them. They included a fossil fish of an extinct species, a 350 year old seashell fossil, and a 13-inch ammonite with opalescent-like iridescence in red-orange hues.

John Davidson

By the time I interviewed John Davidson at the home he shared with his wife Rhonda and assorted children – their daughter Ashleigh and his son John, Jr. and daughter, Jennifer, from a former marriage – he had many movie and television credits. He was then serving as host to a newer version of *Hollywood Squares*. I recalled seeing him in *The Happiest Millionaire* and *The One And Only Genuine Original Family Band* feature films.

The Davidsons were living in the gated Hidden Hills area of Calabasas, west of Los Angeles. Their ranch-style house was comfortably decorated in a style that Rhonda called "Country Eclectic."

I wrote one article that went into quite complete detail of the home's décor. Then I did another dedicated to John's collection of nautical antiques. These were housed and displayed in John's upstairs study, which also contained a case of seashells.

There were turn-of-the-century sextants, telescopes, portlights, binnacles, signal canons, and a Lyle Rescue Gun, which was a small cannon used to shoot a line to some point or to a person in another boat.

"You have to shop in specialty stores for these items and I got many of them on trips to Massachusetts and Connecticut," said John.

On the walls were sailors'"wools" and sailors'"valentines." The former were stitchery pictures fashioned of their own ships by sailors; the latter being handmade shell designs in hardwood frames. These items generally became gifts for the family members that waited for them at home while they were at sea.

Among the group of marine paintings on John's walls was one of his own 96-foot 1928 era classic motor yacht, which was moored up the coast at Oxnard, and which, on another day, I visited with Ralph.

Named the Principia, the boat was, indeed impressive. It had been used as a Presidential yacht in motion pictures and entertained numerous celebrities. Its fixtures included crystal chandeliers, mahogany paneled walls, a wood burning fireplace, garbage disposal, microwave, toaster oven, dishwasher, range with oven, refrigerator, freezers, and modern electronics and power systems. Its entertainment equipment included a jet ski, water ski boat, trap shooting launcher, golf driving pad, ping pong table and pool table.

After giving us a tour, John posed for pictures in its outdoor Jacuzzi.

Timothy Bottoms

I met James "Bud" Bottoms, who was the father of Timothy, Joseph, Samuel, and Ben Bottoms, all actors, before I met his son, Timothy.

The family lived in Santa Barbara and I had spent a day interviewing Bud, a sculptor and art teacher, who was responsible for the life-size Dolphin Family sculpture that graces the Friendship Fountain at the entrance to Stearn's Wharf in downtown Santa Barbara, among other sea mammal sculptures. He told me that he loved to swim with the dolphins and did so regularly. My article about him was published in the Southern California Auto Club Magazine, *Westways.*

On a later day, Ralph and I went to Tim's house to talk with him and his wife, Marcia. Tim had already appeared in a number of movies, including a "small," but complex one, called *"The High Country*, co-starring Linda Purl. I had enjoyed it before I ever met Tim or Linda so it was especially interesting to me now that I knew them both.

Some of his other movies up to that time were *The Paper Chase, Hurricane,* and *The Other Side of the Mountain, Part II.* Other well known actors had given him the enviable accolade of "actor's actor."

The father of four children – one with his first wife and three with Marcia – Tim had portrayed the father figure on *The Land of the Lost* TV series.

Tim told me about a 320 acre ranch farther north in the Big Sur country, of which he was the owner. He said that he kept several horses and some donkeys there for the pleasure of himself and his family, and had plans to lead pack trips and host campers on his scenic land.

Like his dad and brothers, Tim had spent many hours surfing, diving and fishing the Pacific Ocean.

Chapter 61
Our Day with John Forsythe

Back in 1998, when Ralph and I drove up to the beautiful, rolling hills of Santa Ynez Valley to visit John Forsythe, we had no idea that in 2002 he would marry a third wife.

He seemed perfectly content to be living alone on his thirty acre ranch with his only regular company a Japanese housekeeper of 28 years duration. His wife of 51 years had passed away four years before, but he was very involved with the breeding, raising, and racing of Thoroughbred horses and enjoyed occasional visits from his family of three grownup children, six grandchildren, and (at that time) one great-grandchild.

Seated on the closed-in sun porch of his homey hilltop ranch house and gazing out upon a panoramic view of emerald green slopes and a gentle mountain backdrop, he said. "This has been my dream -- to come here; to live here.

"I'm a small town boy," he explained. "I was born in Penns Grove, New Jersey, raised in a small town, and love small town life. My wife, Julie, was a true Los Angeles girl and it took some persuading to get her to move, but she loved it too when we did."

He told us that his house was 65-years-old and had been a

summer home for the famous Pillsbury family. "The name they gave it – El Tesoro – means The Treasure in Spanish."

John gave us a tour of the three bedroom main house and the two-story guest house created from a former goat barn. He showed us his large patio, swimming pool, and old fashioned swing hanging from a tree in front of the house.

We asked John to tell us how he decided to become an actor. He said he had left the University of North Carolina in his junior year to take a job as a sports announcer for the Brooklyn Dodgers at Ebbetts Field.

"Since that was a seasonal occupation, I decided to take a crack at being a radio actor. My father was not very happy about me leaving school anyway so when I told him that I was thinking of becoming an actor, he said 'Hmph' a couple of times.

"I said, 'Something wrong?'

"He said, 'son, I never worried about your sister. I never worried about you. I always thought you could get along. Now I'm worried about you.'

"I asked, 'Why?'

"He said, 'Because you're a nice fellow – a good guy – and you don't look like an actor. You don't sound like an actor. They wear their hats cocked on the side. They talk funny and they walk funny. And they never put their arms through their overcoat. That's not you.'

"I didn't know who he was talking about. Maybe John Barrymore.

"Later, he saw me attain stardom on Broadway, with my name up in lights on the marquee, and it was a big thing."

After his role in the movie *Destination Tokyo* in 1943, John left what was becoming his motion picture career to serve in World

War II, appearing in the U.S. Army Air Forces play and film, *Winged Victory* and working with injured soldiers who had developed speech problems.

At the time of our interview, he was best known for his roles in the TV series *Bachelor Father, Charlie's Angels,* and *Dynasty.* He had more recently appeared as host and narrator of four one-hour documentaries for Turner Broadcasting called *Portrait of Great Britain,* and served as executive producer, director, and host-narrator of a one-hour film documentary of the life and career of legendary jockey Bill Shoemaker, entitled *Nice Guys Finish First.*

Besides informing us about his record breaking and race winning horses, John showed us his Eclipse Award from the National Thoroughbred Association, presented to him in 1988 for his many services rendered to the field of horseracing. Those included serving as Master of Ceremonies at their annual award dinner since 1977.

With full and partial ownership of 14 horses at that time, John told us that five of them were in training at the nearby Flag Is Up Farms belonging to Monty Roberts, known as The Horse Whisperer.

To round out our visit, John took us to that farm to meet Monty Roberts and check out his own dark bay horse named Caracal. I enjoyed riding with John and having more time to talk with him as we led the way in his car, followed by Ralph.

He told me that Monty had learned the horse language that he called Equus by observing wild horses in Nevada as a young boy and that he was able to communicate so well with a horse that had never been touched by a human being he needed just a half hour to have it come to him and allow a rider up on its back. "He has revolutionized the way horses are trained," John said.

Our visit at the farms lasted an hour or so and then John took us to one of his familiar restaurants for lunch, where everyone greeted him like an old friend.

It was easy to see that he was definitely at home in his country setting.

Back at John's ranch, I watched him looking out the window again.

"My pride and my joy is that scenery," he remarked. "I just sit here and watch, and it seems to change from time to time, almost like watching the ocean."

Chapter 62

Some At-Home-with-the-Stars Stories

Mary Frann

Mary Frann is probably best known for her role of Joanna Loudon, the wife of Bob Newhart's character in the 1982 to 1990 version of the TV series *Newhart*. Or maybe for her role of Amanda Howard in the *Days of Our Lives* soap opera (1974 – 1979). And, of course she was America's Junior Miss in 1961.

Looking back on our Mary Frann interview, the one word that seems best in describing her is "meticulous."

Ralph and I had expected to spend a couple of hours at her house, with one hour for me to talk with her and another for him to photograph her in various rooms. Instead we were there for most of an entire day. And it was a good thing for all of us that she had prepared a buffet of food covering her dining room table.

Our assignment was to do an At-Home-With-The-Stars type cover story for *Woman's World* magazine.

When I said "all of us," I was including her hair and makeup people and her agent, all of whom seemed perfectly content to spend their day at her beck and call.

Don't get me wrong. Mary was a very gracious hostess and more than ready to cooperate with the needs of both Ralph and me.

The thing was that for every picture Ralph was prepared to take, she wanted to wear a different outfit and refresh both her makeup and her hairdo. So each of those events took at least a half hour or so of preparation in between.

It was the sort of thing actors run into when filming a movie or TV show. Hurry up so as to be ready for your scene; then wait and wait for all the necessary preparations for shooting it. And this went on and on, over and over.

It was definitely a switch, since we more often ran into interviewees who wanted us out of their house in no more than an hour.

What we had to do here was resign ourselves to the waiting around.

When I finally did get to talk with Mary, I found that "meticulous" was, indeed, one of her major characteristics.

She liked to compare her feelings about fashion in clothes with her views on house decorating.

"I don't like anything to be too formal or too stiff," she said. "I think it's great fun to dress up and feel glamorous and pretty, but everything has to be comfortable as well."

She said that when she hired a designer to help with the planning of the décor of her home she told that person that she had three things in mind.

"I wanted to use pastel colors. I wanted to blend my family keepsakes into the setting. And I wanted a feeling of space and big cushy furniture, nothing diminutive. In choosing my clothes, I like things to be soft and in pastel colors. I like fabrics that move with you."

She said that in the past, her friends called her the Beige Queen because she was known to wear lots of beige and white. "I still love beige and white, but now I wear livelier colors like peach and mauve as well," she reiterated.

Michele Lee

Eventually Ralph and I were to do an At-Home-With-The-Stars story for *Woman's World* magazine on Michele Lee's lovely Los Angeles area home, but our first visit with her was for a different purpose.

(At that time, she was known as "Karen Fairgate MacKenzie on the CBS television series, *Knotts Landing*. My sons, however, knew her best for the role she played in *The Love Bug* motion picture, which featured a talking Volkswagen.)

When Michele Lee's publicist suggested that we do an article on her "collection" for *Collectibles Illustrated*, we weren't certain that it would be appropriate. But, after all, there was really no limit to the type of collections that publication focused upon.

That was why we found ourselves in the actress's upstairs bedroom , helping her to surround herself on her bed with an assortment of more than 50 large photo albums. Blue, brown, tan, red- and fuchsia-flowered, with up-to-100-pages each, they contained views of at least five generations of her family, all her childhood and adult happenings including her career and candid shots of some of the world's most famous celebrities.

"What I really have is a collection of memories," she told us earnestly.

To be certain, they were accurate chronologically, she had all of her negatives catalogued and cross-indexed by dates, events, and personalities.

This painstaking hobby began when she inherited a large batch of loose family photos dating back to her great-grandparents on both sides, following the death of her parents. This heritage involved Russia, England, Poland and, eventually, New York. In bringing order out of what seemed to her "a real mess," she became overly enthusiastic. And she was a stickler for accuracy.

Later, she began taking casual celebrity photos at whatever special events she attended. Examples of these included Princess Grace in an elegant Sable coat standing in line beside actress Julie Harris with her hair in rollers to pick up their tickets for the Night of 100 Stars. Others were a shot of Joan Collins napping, Pam Dawber brushing her teeth, Joyce DeWitt before and after getting "dressed up," and Harry Belefonte standing upon a couch to post a notice on a wall. Her list of candid celebrity pictures went on and on.

"My picture collection is like having a video tape of my life," she concluded with a grin. "When you look at my albums chronologically, you really see little Michele Lee grow up, and with every album, there's another little piece of age there."

Chapter 63
Garland and Grafton

The following two ladies became cover stories for Mature American magazine. Both were outstanding in their own ways.

Actress Beverly Garland

"Running a hotel is a bit like running a small city," said Beverly Garland. And, of course, she knew what she was talking about.

Ralph and I were seated in the office of the large and luxurious Beverly Garland Hotel in North Hollywood, California, interviewing its equally attractive owner and namesake.

Career-wise, Beverly was probably best-known for her roles as Fred MacMurray's wife on the long-running television series My Three Sons and Kate Jackson's mother in Scarecrow and Mrs, King.

But her other activities were just as important, if not more so.

She helped her husband, Fillmore Crank, to run the hotel, served as Honorary Mayor of North Hollywood, represented the National Tour Association, and was Mom and Grandma to her real life family. She was on the Board of Advisors of Toys For Tots and of the California Tourism Corporation, and a member of the Greater

Los Angeles Visitors and Convention Bureau's Board of Directors and a former member of the Bureau's executive committee.

The Santa Cruz, California native had always wanted to act and always kept busy. While training and waiting for her first real break, she had supported herself by waiting tables, operating an elevator, and even sorting the mail at a mortuary. Her motion picture debut was in the 1950 feature film D.O.A. and by the time of our visit, she had over 200 TV and movie roles to her credit.

She was mother to a grownup son and daughter, stepmother to two grownup children, and had six grandchildren and one great-grandchild on the way.

"My hotel is my life," she told us.

Situated on seven acres of tree- and flower-filled park-like grounds, the early California-style edifice had five floors, 248 rooms, meeting rooms, a conference center, ballroom, theater, projection room, dining room, coffee shop, cocktail lounge, heated swimming pool and lighted tennis courts.

With 21 years of running the hotel behind her at that time, Beverly had dozens of employees to do her bidding, but it had not always been that way.

She told us some "horror stories" regarding her business.

"About two weeks before we opened, someone came in and stole three floors of drapes right off the windows. And when the hotel was new, it was a common thing for people to steal television sets because they, too, were all new.

"Another time a man rented a room and after he'd left, we found he'd spray-painted it red. Also, a couple with two children who stayed here for a week, came to the front desk every morning to pay for the next day. On the day they left, they did not come down and pay. Then, when we went into the room, we found they had taken the lamps, bedding, and all sorts of other small items.

"One week – about six months after our opening – the entire staff of maids called in sick with the Asian Flu. Fillmore said to me 'What do you want to do?"

"I said, 'What do you mean?'

"So he elaborated, 'Do you want to clean the rooms and the toilets or do you want to do the laundry?'

"I chose the laundry. So, for a week, I pre-soaked, pre-washed, and washed 400 to 500 sheets and twice as many pillow cases a day, not to mention the towels. Then I'd take them out of the washers and lug them over to the dryers and then I had to fold them." She grimaced. "Folding king-size sheets without dragging them on the floor is not easy when you are doing it all by yourself."

Author Sue Grafton

When Ralph and I went to visit Sue Grafton at her two-story Mediterranean-style Santa Barbara home, I took along a set of colorful wooden children's' blocks bearing letters of the alphabet. The reason? I wanted to use them as a prop when Ralph photographed her.

We sat outside at a picnic table and Sue obligingly stacked the blocks while Ralph snapped his camera.

I was already a great fan of hers, having enjoyed reading all of the books in her "alphabet series' up to that date. By the time I had read about the adventures of her protagonist Private Detective Kinsey Millhone in *A is for Alibi, B Is for Burglar* and *C Is for Corpse,* I was hooked. Now, approximately halfway through the impressive project, Sue told me that when she reached the final book in the series, she would call it *Z Is For Zero*.

Although the stories are set in the fictitious seaside town of Santa Teresa, it is easy to recognize Sue's own real-life hometown of Santa Barbara. And Kinsey's original Volkswagen had been inspired by one once owned by Sue as well.

The Kentucky-born writer had written other novels and a number of screenplays for television movies before beginning her current undertaking.

Sue said that she felt she was following in the footsteps of her father, C.W. Grafton.

"My dad was an attorney, whose specialty was bonds, but to amuse himself in the evenings, he'd go back down to his office and work on mystery novels," she said.

His books included *The Rat Began To Gnaw The Rope* and *The Rope Began to Hang the Butcher*, which Sue believed was intended to be the start of a series based on a nursery rhyme about an old lady trying to get her pig over a stile.

Among many other things Sue told me about her creation of Kinsey Millhone was the following:

"I funnel a lot of my opinions through Kinsey's smart mouth and when I first started doing it in *A Is For Alibi*, I thought 'people are going to get mad at me. I can't say this.' And then I thought 'I'm gonna do it anyway.' And it turns out that those are probably the very things that people relate to, that make people laugh aloud while they're reading these books. So it's turned out to be fun to be slightly outrageous and not have to take the responsibility for her remarks. After all, Kinsey said it – I didn't!"

Chapter 64
Unexpected Artists

While working for Collectibles Illustrated magazine, Ralph and I had occasions to produce stories on people who were creators of collectibles instead of collectors. This had happened with Elke Sommer, for one. Here are a couple of the others.

Jonathan Winters

In the early 1980s, Comedian Jonathan Winters was living in a large home in Toluca Lake and had created a studio in his basement where he worked at turning out colorfully whimsical paintings, many of which had been offered to the public as limited edition lithographs and posters.

On arriving at his home, Ralph and I were privileged to be invited downstairs to talk and take our photos. It was there that we learned that Jon had been a serious art student, studying cartooning and drawing at Dayton Art Institute and had been considering becoming an advertising layout man. But, because he didn't feel that he had developed a particular style all his own at that time, he decided to "table" his art.

Since his talents as a performer were much in demand, he said his painting schedule was often sporadic. He considered himself a part-time sort of guy. "I do a lot of things on a part-time basis and I like it that way," he remarked.

Nevertheless, he had accomplished about 100 paintings as well as a number of movies such as It's a *Mad, Mad, Mad, Mad World*, hosted *The Tonight Show* for two weeks, and appeared in such TV Series as *Mork and Mindy* and *Hollywood Squares*.

Jon showed us some of his pictures. They were delightfully simple, yet kooky with oddly appropriate names. A scene of a giant robin's egg beside a dainty wren's house was entitled Housing Shortage and a group of crazy-quilt colored birds frolicking against a foggy seaside background was labeled The Umbrella Dancers.

"My ideas often begin with a title," he said. "My art is me. It slides in between the worlds of primitive and surrealism. My paintings are as improvisational as my comedy."

Some of the others were *The First and Last Day of Spring*, illustrated with flowering trees and houses on a lush green background with falling bombs promising *imminent disaster*, and *The Land of Hang-ups*, picturing several trees with coat hangers on them.

As of this writing, Jonathan is known to spend some of his spare time being friendly and casually entertaining the general public wherever he may meet them on his shopping rounds in the Santa Barbara and Ventura area, the vicinity where he now lives.

Irish McCalla

The statuesque blond lady Ralph and I interviewed at the 1984 Southern California Association of Plate Collector Clubs' show at the Anaheim Convention Center would have been equally at home if she were wearing the skimpy imitation leopard-skin costume with brief leather shoes and special lion-adorned earrings she was known for in her 1955-56 television portrayal of *Sheena, Queen of the Jungle*.

Actually, the earrings had been abandoned after the pilot because her chimpanzee companion had insisted on yanking them from her ears.

By this time, however, Irish McCalla had made an even more important name for herself as the artist responsible for over 1,000 paintings, eight limited edition collector plates, and numerous offset limited edition lithographs. Her works graced Nixon's Western White House, the Los Angeles Museum of Science and Industry, and the Cowgirl Hall of Fame.

A member of Women Artists of the West, she specialized in western themes involving children, working in watercolors, oils, charcoal, and pastels, as well as sculpting.

"I pretended I was a jungle girl the same as a lot of other kids when I was a child back in Nebraska," she told us, "so when I acted the part of Sheena, it was really like living out a fantasy."

Although her original ambition was to become a professional artist, when she moved to California with an older brother, she became a model for photographers and artists, best known for becoming a Varga Girl poster "pinup" favored by the military.

It was a photographer who suggested her for the part of Sheena after Actress Anita Ekberg failed to show up for the job.

"We spent seven and half months on location down in southern Mexico," she told us.

What brought her home temporarily were injuries received

on crashing into a tree. Ill with dysentery, she was very weak, but still doing her own stunts. From a high level bar, she was attempting to swing in on a vine and knock a bad guy down from the tree. She felt herself slipping and brought her knees up, but ended up with torn ligaments in her left arm and bloodied legs from knee to ankle.

When sent for special medical treatments, it was taken for granted she'd hit the tree while driving a car until she blushingly managed to stammer out the truth.

Irish McCalla had her own McCalla Enterprises, Inc. limited edition plates and prints company and was then living in the mountains above Prescott, Arizona. It was there that she had recently completed a painting of her own 16-month-old grand-daughter, Chelsea McIntyre and daughter-in-law, Kim. The picture was entitled *Blossom Soft* and inspired by the baby's first encounter with peach blossoms.

Epilogue

Times change, and so has the writing business.

When my husband, Bob, and I were first married, he joked that I had married him for his electric typewriter. And, indeed, it had been a step up from my old pink portable manual one.

But then we acquired a computer and that was so much better. No longer did we need carbon paper or white-out to make corrections. With our big printing machine, we could make as many copies as we wanted.

The next step was to send in stories on a disc (if your editor was as modernly equipped as you were).

I'm sad to say that Bob passed away before "going on-line" was a really common thing to do. I had to find my way, without his help, to the point where my stories could be sent to the editor by email

But those were just the mechanical changes.

Over the years of my freelance celebrity article writing career, one fact always stood out. It is that, if a writer hangs around long enough, she or he will find that magazine editors and, indeed, magazines themselves, have a tendency to come and go.

Connections with special editors and magazines that like your work and continue to give you regular assignments – the standard phrase is to count you among their "stable" of writers – are the things that keep a freelancer in business.

I was fortunate enough to make that connection with a wide variety of publications. There were some that closed down after a number of years and others that moved to a new location and changed editors. Then, there were those that simply decided to change the content of their pages.

When *Mature American* magazine, a company-owned publication, ceased to exist, it marked the beginning of the end of my celebrity article writing days. With its single star cover pictures furnished by Ralph and exclusive, well-illustrated personality profiles written by me, it had lured famous "older" stars into welcoming our attention. Once in that door, we had been able to maintain our acquaintance and produce further stories for other publications as well.

Soon, I was spending more time on other sorts of articles, from writing about collectibles to travel to children's self-help to horses and jockeys, to business enterprises, to airplanes and pilots, and, eventually, the military.

Ever flexible, I have endeavored to move on, seek new markets, and switch to writing in different styles and categories.

Index

CPSIA information can be obtained at www.ICGtesting.com
Printed in the USA
LVOW12s2040131213

365206LV00002B/533/P